The Power

of the

Holy Spirit

By
G. Earl Knight

TEACH Services, Inc.
Brushton, New York

ISBN 1-57258-141-7
Library of Congress Catalog Card No. 98-87168

Published by

TEACH Services, Inc.
254 Donovan Road
Brushton, New York 12916

Dedication

This book is dedicated to my wife, Yvonne, who has shared with me twenty-one years of her life in marriage. Her life of devotion to God has inspired me on my Christian pilgrimage.

Table of Contents

Acknowledgment

There are several people who have made great contribution to the publishing of this book that I want to acknowledge. Without the inspiration of Carlton Goodridge to study in this area of the Holy Spirit, this publication would not have been possible. I thank my secretary, Joyce Hospedales, my former secretary, Evelyn Griffin, for their help in preparing the manuscript.

I must acknowledge the untiring efforts of Dr. Rollin Shoemaker, who offered his theological, linguistic and editorial skills in the final preparation of this manuscript. His work was invaluable towards this publication.

Thanks also to my friend, Neville Mujikwa, for his encouragement and support given to this project.

Finally, thanks to the Great I Am for strength, insight and inspiration as I have found a deeper relationship with Him as a result of this work. Praise to the Father, Son, and Holy Spirit.

INTRODUCTION

The study of the Holy Spirit has been the best spiritual experience I ever had. No other subject has ever gripped my attention and devotion as this one. I feel humble as a result of this research because it reveals to me my insufficiencies and my need to totally depend on the Holy Spirit's power. Having a deeper insight into any member of the trinity is a privilege that carries with it a responsibility of conforming one's life to the Divine Character.

Joel 2:28, 29 declares, *And it shall come to pass afterward, that I will pour out my Spirit on all flesh; your sons and your daughters shall prophesy, your old men shall dream dreams, and your young men shall see visions. Even upon the manservant and the maidservants in those days, I will pour out my Spirit.*[1] This had a partial fulfillment[2] on the day of Pentecost. Thus it began a new dispensation—the dispensation of the Holy Spirit.

The Apostles' ministry was accompanied by the presence and power of the Holy Spirit. No wonder they were able to accomplish so much in such a short time. Christ's instruction to his disciples, *And behold, I send the promise of My Father upon you; but stay in the city, until you are clothed with power from on high* (Luke 24:49), was the catalyst for a new era.

During those ten days of waiting in the upper-room, the disciples experienced great transformation of character. Their spiritual insight was sharpened and their passion for souls was intensified, as evidenced in 3,000 souls being baptized.

For the church of God to be effective in these last days, the church must experience the outpouring of the Holy Spirit. God is counting on us to rise up and proclaim His

---

[1] All quotations from Scripture will be from the Revised Standard Version unless otherwise indicated.

[2] The final fulfillment will take place just prior to Christ's second coming.

warming message to a dying world. This, however, cannot be accomplished without the indwelling presence of the Holy Spirit in the life of the believer. It is the Holy Spirit that must ignite the believer into action to be a witness in and to the world.

As we await the second coming of Jesus Christ, we are called upon to go forth and proclaim the gospel message to the world. Christ puts it plainly when he said, *Go therefore and make disciples of all nations, baptizing them in the name of the Father and of the Son and of the Holy Spirit, teaching them to observe all that I have commanded you; and lo, I am with you always, to the close of the age* (Matt 28:19–20). It is impossible for this commission to be fulfilled without the power of the Holy Spirit. That is the reason Christ promised the Spirit's power in the gospel proclamation that results in the transformation of sinners.

As Christians, we need the daily baptism of the Holy Spirit so that we may receive power to obey the will of God. Ever since I received this baptism, my life has never been the same.

I would recommend to the readers of these pages to take time to understand this subject and then apply it to yourself. For it is not until the personal application is made that one can benefit experientially.

Chapter One

Who Is the Holy Spirit?

Through the centuries the Holy Spirit has been examined and reexamined, but there is much more room for examination of this profound subject. In the next several pages of this chapter, we will focus on the personality of the Holy Spirit. I would counsel the reader, however, that in an attempt to shed light on this subject, it is impossible to completely comprehend it. The Holy Spirit is an eternal, infinite Being, which means it is impossible for our finite minds to fully comprehend Him.

The Personality of the Holy Spirit

Even from the outset, speaking of the personality of the Holy Spirit will pose some difficulties. The term "person" does not adequately describe Him. He is not a person in the humanistic sense. However, in describing the Holy Spirit, we will acknowledge some human characteristics. Spurgeon and Campbell have concluded that there are four basic components to a human personality: will, intelligence, power, and the capacity to love (*Understanding the Holy Spirit*, 10). While these components may be limited in finite human beings, they are unlimited in a Divine Being such as the Holy Spirit.

Mankind is circumscribed by his human limitations. Mankind came from the hand of God clothed in a veil of humanity with limitations. The Holy Spirit, predating mankind, co-existed with God from everlasting to everlasting. So as we investigate the personality of the Holy Spirit,

1

let us not limit Him only to our finite understanding, but leave room for the wide experience of infinite wisdom.

"In the third century of the Christian era, Paul of Samosata advanced a theory denying the Divinity of Christ and regarding the Holy Spirit as an influence, as an exertion of a Divine energy and power" (*Understanding the Holy Spirit*, 11). This theory eventually lost steam as the centuries progressed. But around the time of the reformation, two men, Laelius Socinus and his nephew, Faustus Socinus, revived the theory. Unfortunately, many of the people accepted it. It came to be known as Socinianism. This theory had an impact on Christendom. There are many people today who speak of the Holy Spirit as an "It" and see Him as an influence or force, not as a person.

In the Gospel of John it is recorded, *When the Spirit of truth comes, he will guide you into all the truth; for he will not speak on his own authority, but whatever he hears he will speak, and he will declare to you the things that are to come* (John 16:13). Although the Greek word *pneuma* (spirit) used here is neuter, it is in opposition to the Greek word *ekeinos* (that one) which is masculine. Hence it is proper to refer to the Holy Spirit as a "He" and not an "it."

The Gospel of John also makes reference to the Holy Spirit as a "Counselor." *But the Counselor, the Holy Spirit, whom the Father will send in my name, he will teach you all things, and bring to your remembrance all that I have said to you* (John 14:26). The Greek word for counselor is *paraklete*. It is composed of the preposition *para*, meaning "beside," and the adjective *kletis* meaning "called." Thus the meaning of the word, *parakletis*, could literally be "the one who is called to the side of." The Holy Spirit is the "Helper," the "Intercessor" and "Advocate," the One who is called to our side, the One summoned to help us.

In the gospel of John chapters 14 through 16, Jesus spoke extensively of the Holy Spirit and His personal relationship with Him. In His discourse Jesus never used a word or phrase that would indicate that the Holy Spirit is a force, or power, or an influence, i.e., Jesus never said anything that would indicate that the Holy Spirit is person-alityless. Jesus clearly states that, He shall teach, He shall bear witness, He shall convict, He shall guide (John 14:26; 15:26; 16: 8, 13), all characteristics of a personality. These characteristics do not suggest an influence, power, or force devoid of intellect or intelligence. These characteristics are descriptive of a personality.

Scripture not only teaches that the Holy Spirit has a personality but that He is a divine person. In the book of Isaiah we read: *And I said: "Woe is me! For I am lost; for I am a man of unclean lips, and I dwell in the midst of a people of unclean lips; for my eyes have seen the King, the LORD of hosts!" And he said, "Go, and say to this people: 'Hear and hear, but do not understand; see and see, but do not perceive' "* (Isa 6:5,9). In vision, the prophet Isaiah had come into the presence of the Divine and saw how undone or imperfect he himself was. In the New Testament there is an exposition of that vision by Isaiah. (Acts 28:25–26.) *So, as they disagreed among themselves, they departed, after Paul had made one statement: "The Holy Spirit was right in saying to your fathers through Isaiah the prophet: 'Go to this people, and say, You shall indeed hear but never understand, and you shall indeed see but never perceive.' "* According to Luke, Paul says that it was the Holy Spirit who uttered these words which Isaiah said were spoken by God. The New Testament's use of the Old Testament here, reveals the Divinity of the Holy Spirit.

The work attributed to the Holy Spirit is the work of Divinity. Genesis declares that God by means of the Holy Spirit created the cosmos out of chaos (Genesis 1:2). In the gospel of John it is stated that the baptism of the Holy Spirit must accompany the new birth experience. Paul declares that our mortal bodies will be quickened by the Holy Spirit (Romans 8:11). The works of creation, regeneration and resurrection, are brought about by Divinity. The Holy Spirit, as described in Genesis, is the agent through which God creates and recreates. Thus the Holy Spirit is not only a person but a Divine person carrying out the cooperative will of the Godhead.

The Holy Spirit possesses the Divine attributes of God: He has all power (Genesis 1:2; Job 33:4; Ps 104:30), all knowledge (John 14:26; 1 Corinthians 2:10, 11), and He is omnipresent, being present everywhere at the same time (Psalm 139:7–10).

The Holy Spirit is very crucial to our understanding of the plan of salvation. Each member of the Godhead has a distinct role in the salvation of mankind. The Holy Spirit's role is indispensable to our salvation. For it is He who leads our souls to salvation in Christ Jesus. *For all who are led by the Spirit of God are sons of God* (Romans 8:14). It is because of His attributes that He is able to represent our needs to God with groaning that cannot be uttered (Romans 8:26). As far as we sinners are concerned, the Holy Spirit's workings are indispensable to our salvation.

The scriptures speak of the Holy Spirit as being active in the life of the believer. Many references definitely rule out the idea that the Holy Spirit is a mere influence, power or force: the Holy Spirit hears and speaks (John 16:13, Matt 10:20; Acts 13:2), consults (John 16:8); imparts love (Romans 5:5); equips individuals for special kinds of services (Exodus 21:2; 35:31); encourages (Acts 9:31), transforms (II Corinthians 3:18); consecrates for ministry (Acts 20:28), and leads (Romans 8:14).

Ellen White wrote: "The Holy Spirit is a person, for He beareth witness with our spirits that we are the children of God. When this witness is borne, it carries with it its own evidence. As such we believe and are sure that we are the children of God" (Evangelism, 616). Hence the Holy Spirit has a personality that is advantageous for humanity. Not only does He sympathize with us in our sinful condition but He is able to empathize with us and lead us out of the valleys of sin to the mountain top experience of Christ's righteousness. The Holy Spirit abides with us as a companion. If we listen to His counsels, our minds will be constantly guarded and guided in the right path and our actions will always meet with God's approval.

Chapter Two

The Holy Spirit and the Trinity

The doctrine of the trinity cannot be easily explained. In fact, it took the Early Church 300 years to see its declaration in Scriptures. God had never set about to prove His mode of existence. As much as we might use the different phenomena of nature as physical imagery to explain God, we fall far short in articulating the attributes of the Godhead. In the book of Job the question is raised, *Can you find out the deep things of God? Can you find out the limit of the Almighty?* (Job 11:7).

Our finite minds cannot comprehend the infinite God. He is higher than heavens, wider than oceans, deeper than the seas, yet God has revealed Himself to us through His Son and through the activities of His Holy Spirit. His revelations began at creation and will continue to the second coming of Christ. All through the history of mankind God has revealed Himself to man. Unfortunately man has fallen short in understanding God and accepting His revelations.

It was during Jesus' ministry on earth when *Philip said to him, "Lord, show us the Father, and we shall be satisfied." Jesus said to him, "Have I been with you so long, and yet you do not know me, Philip? He who has seen me has seen the Father; how can you say, 'Show us the Father'?Do you not believe that I am in the Father and the Father in me? The words that I say to you I do not speak on my own authority; but the Father who dwells in me does his works"* (John 14:8–10).

The plurality of the Godhead is found in the first book of the Bible. *In the beginning God created the heavens and the earth* (Genesis 1:1). The expression used in Hebrew for God is *elohim*, which is a plural form, meaning three or more, suggesting that the Godhead has more than two members. The second verse amplifies the first by stating, *The earth was without form and void, and darkness was upon the face of the deep; and the Spirit of God was moving over the face of the waters* (Genesis 11:2). At the creation of the world, we see the Holy Spirit in operation.

On the sixth day of creation week God said: *Let us make man in our image, after our likeness; and let him have dominion over the fish of the sea, and over the birds of the air, and over the cattle, and over all the earth, and over every creeping thing that creeps upon the earth* (Genesis 1:26). There can be no doubt that the Godhead, i.e., Father, Son , and Holy Spirit were active in creation, and it is logical for one to think that they are active in the recreation of the image of God in mankind in the present day situation. The New Testament throws further light on the subject by stating that: *all things were made through him, and without him was not anything made that was made* (John 1:3). This refers to the Word, the eternal Son, in creation as He cooperates with the Father and the Holy Spirit.

Isaiah, who is referred to as the gospel prophet, records an astonishing prophetic reference: *Draw near to me, hear this: from the beginning I have not spoken in secret, from the time it came to be I have been there. And now the Lord GOD has sent me and his Spirit* (Isa 48:16). In the King James Version this same passage says: *The Lord God, and his Spirit, hath sent me.* The "me" here is referring to the coming One, Jesus Christ, the Messiah, the Deliverer, the Son of God, our Saviour. The KJV makes it appear as if Christ was to be sent by the Father and the Holy Spirit. This inference is not consistent with the prophet. In the RSV it articulates correctly not only the prophecy of the coming of Christ but also the inauguration of the dispensation of the Holy Spirit.

The coming of Christ, the Redeemer, and the Holy Spirit, the Counselor, are fulfillments of prophecy. These prophecies had timely fulfillment in the birth, life, and death of Jesus Christ. His death and subsequent resurrection gave rise to the full working of the Holy Spirit. Today as believers, we can enjoy the full benefit of this promise by constantly submitting our lives to Christ and making room for the operation of the Spirit.

The New Testament has taken up the melody and amplified its sound: *And when Jesus was baptized, he went up immediately from the water, and behold, the heavens were opened and he saw the Spirit of God descending like a dove, and alighting on him, and lo, a voice from heaven saying, "This is my beloved Son, with whom I am well pleased"* (Matthew 3:16–17). The Father in heaven renders His approval by announcing throughout the heavens, even to the earth, that He was satisfied with the baptism of His Son when the Spirit of God descended on Him, anointing Him for the ministry that was yet before him. What solidarity, what unity, what co-union. This is a manifestation of the personality of the Godhead. It was significant that at the beginning of the public ministry of Jesus, there was such a manifestation of the unity of the trinity for the benefit of humanity.

Throughout Christ's earthly ministry, He made reference to the Father and the Holy Spirit. Frequently He made reference to the relationship that exists among them. None may be more pronounced than the great commission itself: *Go therefore and make disciples of all nations baptizing them in the name of the Father and of the Son and of the Holy Spirit* (Matthew 28:19). The phrase "of the" in each case clearly marks the separation of each personality, but the singular reference of "the name" which preface each Deity brings to light the unity of the Godhead. This baptismal formula brings to sharp focus the pre-eminence Christ has given to the unity of the Trinity. In one essential Godhead there co-exists three Persons, co-substantial, co-equal and co-eternal (*Understanding the Holy Spirit*, 20).

Ellen White declared, "There are three living persons of the heavenly trio; in the name of these three great powers—the Father, the Son and the Holy Spirit—those who receive Christ by living faith are baptized, and these powers will co-operate with the obedient subjects of heaven in these efforts to live the new life in Christ" (*Evangelism*, 615).

The Holy Spirit is always spoken of as the third person of the Godhead. Does that mean that He is third in rank? God forbid! No! He is equal with God the Father and God the Son in all things. He is one with the Father and the Son. As the Godhead is revealed throughout history, it seems that the Father was the supreme point. The Jewish people clearly accepted this fact. Then came the revelation of the Son, the Messiah, and after that came the revelation of the Holy Spirit. All three members of the Godhead have been at work since creation. As history unfolds, there seems to be a personal pre-eminence for each member. Since the death of Christ on the cross of Calvary and His ascension to Glory the Holy Spirit has been representing God the Father and the Son on the earth. John 16:8–13 bears out the fact that the Holy Spirit is fully at work and we are living now in the dispensation of the Holy Spirit. Ellen White said, "The dispensation in which we are now living is to be, to those who ask, the dispensation of the Holy Spirit" (*Testimonies to Ministers*, 51).

In Scripture it is distinctly stated that the Spirit is *sent from the Father* (John 14:26) in fulfillment of prophecy, *and now the Lord God has sent me and the Spirit* (Isaiah 48:16). There is an order in the Divine realm and it should not be revised by the finite.

The term "third" must be used with careful limitation. When used with reference to the Godhead, we cannot interpret it as third in rank so that it implies any form of inferiority. The term third has no reference to time or position, but in sequence of revelation. When dealing with divine things, time has very little significance for time has no place in the eternal Being who spun space and time. Campbell and Spurgeon rightly said, "The relation of the Spirit to the Father is declared in the words: *The spirit proceedeth from the Father* (Jonn 15:26)." He is the gift and outpouring of the Divine essence, the eternal Spirit. This defies analysis. It is a truth declared which remains an impenetrable mystery. Man cannot discover that which is not revealed. It is the simple declaration of the word of God, that the Spirit proceedeth from the father; and there the matter must be left.

The relationship of the Spirit to the Son is clearly revealed. In the gospel of John it is stated, *But the Counselor, the Holy Spirit, whom the Father will send in my name, he will teach you all things, and bring to your remembrance all that I have said to you* (John 14:26). The Holy Spirit occupies the place of Christ on earth, revealing the Father and the Son. He quickens and enables the sinner to find acceptance with God through Jesus Christ for the salvation of his soul. What a marvelous relationship, what a mystery, what joy to the sinner to know that all three members of the Godhead are working for his salvation.

God is a mystery and the unity of the Godhead is a mystery. Human language cannot unfold this mystery. But let us walk in the light which has been shed on our way. There is *one* God. There are three persons that form the unity of the Godhead. Each person has His own identity and position in the affairs of Divinity. All three function in the affairs of humanity to restore us to the state before the fall. Let us praise God for His interest in saving us from the ruins of sin.

Chapter Three

The Working of the
Holy Spirit Before the Cross

If anyone thirst, let him come to me and drink. He who believes in me, as the scripture has said, "Out of his heart shall flow rivers of living water." Now this he said about the Spirit, which those who believe in him were to receive; for as yet the Spirit had not yet been given, because Jesus was not yet glorified. (John 7:37–39).

This passage has posed difficulty to some readers, because they believed that Christ was saying that prior to His glorification the Spirit had no role on this earth. This opinion is obviously incorrect. The Old Testament contains many passages where the Holy Spirit is directly mentioned: Genesis 1:2 (creation), Genesis 6:3 (*My Spirit shall not abide in man forever.*), Genesis 41:38 (Pharaoh recognized that the Spirit of God dwelt in Joseph the servant of God), Numbers 27:18 (Joshua was chosen to succeed Moses because in him dwelt the Spirit of God), I Samuel 10:10 (*the Spirit of God came mightily upon* [Saul] *and he prophesied.*), and, Zach 4:6 (*not by might, nor by power, but by my Spirit, says the Lord of host*). So what did John mean, then, when he said, *for as yet the Spirit had not yet been given, because Jesus had not yet been glorified* (7:39). Is the guiding of the Spirit tied to Jesus' glorification?

Jesus was glorified at the cross. His death on Calvary brought sadness to the disciples. Great mourning was among them because they believed their hopes of deliverance from Roman domination were dashed and their desire for self glorification ruined. Jesus, however, was glorified on the cross through His death. He found life not just for

11

Himself, but for sinners who are worthy of death because of their sin. Christ was glorified when He gained victory over sin and death, when He became the second Adam, setting an example for us, gaining the victory for us.

Through the cross Christ was glorified. After His death, He ascended to His Father in heaven and received the Divine approval of a job well done. The plan of redemption was crowned by His death on Calvary and resurrection from the grave. Now room was created for the full operation of the Holy Spirit. Jesus said to His disciples prior to His death, *Now is the Son of man glorified, and in him God is glorified; if God is glorified in him, God will also glorify him in himself, and glorify him at once* (John 13:31-32). It was not very long after He said these words, in fact, during the same evening, Jesus prayed, *Father, the hour has come; glorify thy Son that the Son may glorify thee* (John 17:1).

Jesus also, said, *Nevertheless I tell you the truth: it is to your advantage that I go away, for if I do not go away, the Counselor will not come to you; but if I go, I will send him to you. And when he comes, he will convince the world concerning sin and righteousness and judgment* (John 16:7, 8). Jesus told His disciples that they would not be left alone, but they would receive the personal presence of the Holy Spirit in His fullness after He ascended to His Father. The Counselor, the Advocate, or Comforter is the Holy Spirit, who is promised to the disciples to take the place of Jesus' presence on earth.

The Holy Spirit at Work in Creation

Before the world was created and that which is seen was made out of things which do not appear (Heb 11:3), when this world laid in chaos, God's Spirit was moving over the face of the deep (Genesis 1:3). As Job said, *The Spirit of God has made me, and the breath of the Almighty gives me life* (Job 33:4).

The Holy Spirit was not only involved in creation, but He also sustains it. He watches over His own. Isaiah pondered this matter when he asked the question *who has* directed the Spirit of the Lord, or as his counselor has instructed him? Whom did he consult for his enlightenment, and who taught him the path of justice, and taught him knowledge, and showed him the way of understanding? Behold, the nations are like a drop from a bucket and are accounted as the dust from the scales; behold he takes up the isles like fine dust (Isaiah 40:13–15).

The Holy Spirit has been on constant watch over God's creatures and creation. David further exclaimed, *Whither shall I go from thy Spirit? Or whether shall I flee from thy presence? If I ascend to heaven thou are there! If I make my bed in Sheol, thou art there! If I take the wings of the morning and dwell in the utmost part of the sea, even there thy hand shall lead me, and thy right hand shall hold me* (Psalm 139:7–10). The Spirit of the Lord will pursue even those who attempt to evade him. The Psalmist was glad that the Holy Spirit was always there for him. Aren't we glad that it is impossible to escape the overseeing, controlling, continuing ministry of the Holy Spirit? Isaiah, the gospel prophet, made a profound statement, *When the enemy shall come in like a flood, the Spirit of the Lord shall lift up a standard against him* (Isaiah 59:19). How often in the Old Testament did this happen? Numerous times the Holy Spirit intervened on the behalf of God's servants. Joseph, Moses, Joshua, Esther, David, Daniel and many others were delivered from their enemies. Thank God for the working of His Spirit in times past. His Spirit is even more at work now and is available to all who will accept His protection and leading. Erwin R. Gaine said in his book *Enlightened by the Spirit* "When as individuals we are harassed by temptation and trials, the Holy Spirit is ready at our beckoning to come to rescue" (37).

The Holy Spirit Has Been
a Guide to Patriarchs of Old

In Genesis 6:3, it is stated that *My Spirit shall not abide in man forever*. This is a revealing statement. Remember that the Holy Spirit took part in the creation of this world, and He also took part in the creation of Adam (Genesis 1:26). It grieved the heart of God when man succumbed to the temptation of Lucifer.

God did not delay in providing a way out of sin for man. In fact, God's immediate response to the enemy of souls was, *I will put enmity between you and the woman, and between your seed and her seed; he shall bruise your head, and you shall bruise his heel* (Genesis 3:15). There is no doubt that this promise was in reference to the coming Messiah who would put an end to the dominance of sin in the lives of mankind. Jesus, the Redeemer, would come and conquer Satan and set His people free so that they might serve Him.

The Devil did not hesitate to use all his available forces. He began immediately attacking Adam, Eve, and their descendants. Cain failed to obey the voice of God, and he killed his brother Abel. (Genesis 4: 1–15).

A third son was born to Adam and Eve. They named him Seth. While Cain strayed from the counsel of God and became the father of a rebellious nation, Seth, like his brother Abel, followed the counsel of God. However, Genesis 6: 1,2, states that when man began to multiply on the face of the ground, and daughters were born to them, *the sons of God saw that the daughters of men were fair; and they took to wife such as of them as they chose.*

The descendants of Cain followed the rebellious life of their father and sought after worldly possessions and forsook the promise of God to restore Eden. They disregarded God and His purpose for humanity. Seth and his descendants followed in the lifestyle of Abel. They feared God and followed in ways of righteousness. The two groups of people remained separate as they followed two distinct paths. But as time passed, the two groups commingled, resulting in tragedy. Ellen White said, "So long as their separation continued, they (Seth and his descendants) maintained the worship of God in its purity. But in the lapse of time they ventured little by little, to mingle with the inhabitants of the valleys. This association was productive of the worst results. The children of Seth, attracted by the daughters of Cain's descendants, displeased the Lord by intermarrying with them. Many of the worshipers of God were beguiled into sin by the allurements that were now constantly before them, and they lost their peculiar, holy character. Mingled with the depraved, they became like them in spirit and deeds; the restrictions of the seventh commandment were disregarded, and they took them wives of all which they chose! The children of Seth *'went in the way of Cain'* (Jude 11). They fixed their minds upon worldly prosperity and enjoyment, and neglected the commandments of the Lord. Sin spread abroad in the earth like a deadly leprosy" (*Patriarchs and Prophets*, 81, 82).

This gross spiritual decline resulted in God withdrawing His Spirit from the earth. *My spirit shall not abide with man forever* (Genesis 6:3). This was a sad omen resulting in mankind's total and complete rebellion against God. Even though Noah was chosen by God to witness for 120 years and build the ark as a place of refuge, only eight people were saved when the flood came. In spite of the fact that the Spirit of God was prompting the antediluvian world to turn to God, the vast majority turned their backs on God.

As Moses led the Israelites out of Egypt, God was there with him to guide him in his way. He could not have done it alone. The Prophet Isaiah noted, *Then he remembered the days of old, of Moses his servant. Where is he who brought up out of the sea the shepherds of his flock? Where is he who put in the midst of them his holy spirit, who caused his glorious arm to go at the right hand of Moses, who divided the waters before them to make for himself an everlasting name, who led them through the depths? Like a horse in the desert, they did not stumble. Like cattle that go down into the valley, the Spirit of the Lord gave them rest, so thou didst lead thy people to make for thyself a glorious name* (Isaiah 63:11–14).

The journey from Egypt to Canaan was a treacherous one. Moses faced many tests. Even though he was not always victorious, he trusted in God and the Holy Spirit guided his footsteps through the wilderness.

David, who was known as a *man after God's own heart* (1 Samual 13:14), fell into sin. The prophet Nathan pointed out his sin and in humility David prayed to God, *Cast me not away from thy presence, and take not thy Holy Spirit from me* (Psalm. 51:11). David lost the controlling influence of the Holy Spirit when he fell into sin by stealing another man's wife, and by sending that man to die in battle. When David saw how wretched he himself was, he quickly sought spiritual renewal by confessing to God his sin and by pleading with God that the Holy Spirit would not be taken from him.

The Holy Spirit's work before the cross is well documented in the Old Testament. His role was just as important then as it is now. He was present to intercede, to direct, and to guide as needed. He was there.

"During the patriarchal age the influence of the Holy Spirit had often been revealed in marked manner, but never in its fullness" (*Acts of the Apostles*, 37).

The prophets of the Old Testament depended on the Holy Spirit for guidance as they looked through the telescope of time. As Peter stated, *first of all you must understand this, that no prophecy of scripture is a matter of one's own interpretation, because no prophecy ever come by the impulse of man but men moved by the Holy Spirit spoke of God* (II Peter 2:20, 21).

Joel was one of those prophets who was moved by the Holy Spirit, *And it shall come to pass afterward, that I will pour out my Spirit on all flesh; your sons and your daughters shall prophesy, your old men shall dream dreams, and your young men shall see vision. Even upon the man servants and maid servants in those days I will pour out my Spirit* (Joel 2:28, 29). This prophetic utterance was partially fulfilled on the day of Pentecost. Even now, those who are willing to receive the Holy Spirit, God is ready to in-fill.

Campbell and Spurgeon concluded, "The Spirit of God was the Spirit of communion while sin worked itself out from the fall of man to the flood; He was a Spirit of detailed service while the people of God were being organized into a nation; He was a Spirit of strength while the people were fighting for the land, and were casting out those who had deeply sinned; and He became a Spirit of hope when the peculiar people had passed into a condition of apostasy and wandering. He lit the horizon with a glow of approaching day. He spoke to ears that listened, and revealed to eyes that gazed; and thus, though they did not perfectly understand, men had some dim foreshadowing of the glories of these days of fullness of spiritual power" (*Understanding the Holy Spirit*, 57).

Chapter Four

The Holy Spirit and Christ

The Holy Spirit Promised Christ's Birth

She was young, innocent, and a virgin. She was betrothed to Joseph of the house of David. She had never slept with a man, yet she was to bear a Son whose name was to be called *Jesus, for he shall save his people from their sins* (Matt: 1:21). Mary was her name. She had the honor of being visited by the angel Gabriel, who was sent from God to her in Nazareth. The angel announced, *Hail, oh favored one, the Lord is with you!* (Luke 1:28). Mary was filled with trepidation, but the angel did not leave, he continued by saying, *"Do not be afraid, Mary, for you have found favor with God. And behold, you will conceive in your womb and bear a son and you shall call his name Jesus..."* (Luke 1:30, 31).

This phenomenon brought great concern to Joseph. He planned to denounce Mary quietly. But the angel also appeared to him and said, *do not fear to take Mary as your wife, for that which is conceived in her is of the Holy Spirit* (Matthew 1:20). This was an unprecedented experience for Mary and Joseph. They were amazed at the honor granted to them by God. Yet they themselves did not understand it. They accepted it by faith in the God of their fathers. The angel further said, *The Holy Spirit will come upon you, and the power of the most high will overshadow you; therefore, the child to be born will be called holy, the Son of God* (Luke 1:35).

The human mind cannot fathom this mystery. All the modern computer technology cannot unravel this phenomenon. But, truly it took place and Jesus was born in fulfillment of the announcement. Christ is a Holy Child, the Son of God and man, born of a sinful woman, yet conceived by God through the Holy Spirit. Who can understand this? It is beyond a finite mind to comprehend. Jesus Christ was born of the Spirit, so we must be born of the Spirit if we are to enter the Kingdom of Heaven, (John 3:5).

Albert B. Simpson, a nineteenth century preacher said, "The mystery of the incarnation is repeated every time a soul is created anew in Christ Jesus. Into the unholy being of a child of Adam, a seed of incorruptible and eternal life is implanted by the Divine Spirit, and that seed is in itself, the range, the life of God, holy and incorruptible" (*The Holy Spirit*, 308).

Those who go through the experience of rebirth in the Spirit have received the incorruptible seed of righteousness. John said, *No one born of God commits sin; for God's nature abides in him, and he cannot sin because he is born of God* (1 John 3:9). When the Holy Spirit dwells in us, we cannot continue in sin. Sin becomes distasteful. There is no comfort in that environment anymore. The new birth brings on a new person and a new Spirit is in control now.

From His childhood to His baptism at the age of thirty, the Holy Spirit did not leave Jesus. The Spirit of God was always with Him through His human development. The Holy Spirit was a constant reminder to Jesus as to who He was and for what reason He was born. Mary and Joseph were good parents, but the Holy Spirit was a close companion of Jesus. He was not just another child growing up in Nazareth, but a God-child with a clear mission for the world. "All the progress in the Holy child's advancement in knowledge and holiness must be ascribed unto the Spirit" (Arthur W. Pink, *The Holy Spirit*, 28).

Christ's life was always in connection with the Father, and it was the Holy Spirit that provided the connection. Arthur Pink further states, "It was the Spirit who formed Christ's human nature, and directed the whole tenor of His earthly life. Nothing was undertaken but by the Spirit's directing, nothing was spoken, but by His guidance, nothing executed but by His power" (*The Holy Spirit*, 29).

The Holy Spirit at Christ's Baptism.

When Christ was about to enter His public ministry, He went to John the Baptist who was baptizing people in the Jordan River. He requested of John that He should be baptized by him. John refused because he felt unworthy. Jesus insisted saying, *Let it be so now, for thus it is fitting for us to fulfill all righteousness* (Matthew 3:15).

Without delay, John proceeded to baptize Jesus. Something miraculous took place that day, different from all the previous experiences of John. John saw the Holy Spirit descended upon Jesus like a dove and heard a voice from heaven saying, *This is my beloved Son with whom I am well pleased* (Matthew 3:17).

Here at the commencement of Christ's public ministry, the divine Trio acted in unison. Christ's ministry was publicly acknowledged by the Father in heaven and by the Holy Spirit who descended from heaven. Christ did not doubt whether He had the approval of His Father in heaven or the Holy Spirit, but their declaration at His baptism was a welcomed assurance. Those who looked on must have experienced the moving feeling of the presence of God manifested in all three persons.

Christ's baptism was also an example for us sinners. For it teaches that being born of the water and the Spirit is essential for those who are on the road of salvation. It was Nicodemus, a ruler of the Jews, who came to Jesus by night and said to him, *Rabbi, we know thou art a teacher come from God, for no one can do these signs that you do, unless God is with him.* (John 3: 2). Nicodemus, seemingly, wanted to engage Jesus in some scientific discussion on reproduction when he asked Jesus, *How can a man be born when he is old? Can he enter a second time into his mother's womb and be born? Jesus answered, "Truly, Truly, I say to you, unless one is born of the water and of the Spirit he cannot enter the kingdom of God* (John 3: 4, 5).

Jesus was not demanding of His followers anything that He was not prepared to do. Even though He had no sin, yet He was baptized with water and with the Holy Spirit. Every

21

child of God must have such an experience. There is a Jordan baptism for everyone. A place to meet Jesus and surrender your life to Him. In baptism you bury your past sinful life and unite in oneness with Christ. The weight of sin is cast off and a new life of faith begins. This water baptism must be accompanied by the baptism of the Holy Spirit for it is only then that a sinner can be regenerated with the ability to lead a new life with Christ.

Christ's Ministry Was Led
And Empowered By The Holy Spirit

The Bible says that very soon after His baptism, *Jesus, full of the Holy Spirit, returned from the Jordan, and was led by the Spirit for forty days in the wilderness, tempted by the devil* (Luke 4:1, 2). At the commencement of His public ministry, Christ's faith was immediately put to the test. Albert Simpson said, "Forty days His blessing was challenged, His faith tested and His very soul tried by all the assault of the adversary" (*The Holy Spirit*, 311).

Satan was a witness to Christ's baptism. He witnessed the glory of God overshadowing Jesus as the voice from heaven declared, *This is my beloved son, with whom I am well pleased* (Matthew 3:17). He, Satan, witnessed the Holy Spirit descending on Jesus the Son of God. How jealous Satan must have been. Satan must have made a vow that day to destroy Jesus at any price.

Christ was led into the wilderness by the Spirit. He fasted and prayed. Jesus needed strength from His Father to meet the challenges that were before Him. He needed this time with God. He needed to be spiritually charged to be adequately prepared for the race ahead. The Devil would not let Him alone. The Devil came with his barrage of temptations to abort the salvation plan of Jesus. Jesus, with total dependence on His Father, conquered the evil one.

The human race was to be redeemed by Christ, so He had to overcome sin as one of us. Adam succumbed to the temptation of the devil. The devil constantly, "points to Adam's sin as proof that God's law was unjust, and could not be obeyed" (*Desire of Ages*, 117). In humanity Christ was to redeem Adam's failure. He could not face the devil as God for then He could not be our example. He had to face the devil as a mere man with the possibility of sinning. "When Adam was assailed by the tempter, none of the effects of sin were upon him. He stood in the strength of perfect manhood, possessing the full vigor of mind and body. He was surrounded with the glories of Eden, and was in daily communion with heavenly beings. It was not thus with Jesus when He entered the wilderness to cope with Satan. For four thousand years the race had been decreasing in physical strength, in mental power, and in moral worth; and Christ took upon Himself the infirmities of degenerate humanity. Only thus could He rescue man from the lowest depths of his degeneration" (*Desire of Ages*, 117).

Jesus Christ met Satan in the power of the Spirit. This same power is available for us to have as we meet Satan daily. "Our Saviour took humanity with all its liabilities. He took the nature of man, with the possibility of yielding to temptation" (*Desire of Ages*, 117). Yet He never sinned, He did not allow Satan to place doubt in His mind about who He was or whose He was. Christ faced the devil's most vicious temptations. He never failed. *For we have not a high priest who is unable to sympathize with our weaknesses, but one who in every respect has been tempted as we are, yet without sin* (Heb. 4:13). Because He overcame we can also overcome through Him.

Temptations will come our way. As long as we are in this world we will have to encounter the adversary of our soul. The same Spirit who led Jesus into the wilderness was with Him throughout the forty days of intense trial. The Spirit that led Him into the wilderness also led Him out. God will never leave us nor forsake us. He will be with us through every trial. If we trust Him, victory is assured. Isaiah said, *When you pass through the waters I will be with you, and through the rivers, they shall not overwhelm you. When you walk through the fire, you shall not be burned, and the flame shall not consume you* (Isaiah 43:2).

Let us not fear the conflict; let us not be weary of the trials that come upon us. The Lord will be above us to watch over us, beneath us, to uphold us, before us to guide us and behind us to protect us. *When the enemy shall come in like a flood, the Spirit of the Lord shall lift up a standard against him* (Isaiah 59:19).

The scripture says that after the temptation of Jesus in the wilderness, *Jesus returned in the power of the Spirit into Galilee, and a report concerning him went out throughout all the surrounding country* (Luke 4:14). Christ was not weakened by the wilderness experience, but strengthened. His faith was not shaken but was made stronger. He overcame the devil himself, not with His own strength, but with great reliance on the Word of God.

Jesus soon went back to His home town *where He had been brought up; and he went to the synagogue, as his custom was, on the Sabbath day. And he stood up to read.* Having been given the book of the prophet Isaiah He opened to the passage. *"The Spirit of the Lord is upon me, because He has anointed me to preach good news to the poor. He has sent me to proclaim release to the captives and recovering of sight to the blind, to set at liberty those who are oppressed, to proclaim the acceptable year of the Lord"* (Luke 4:18, 19).

All the works of Jesus, all His miracles, all His teachings, were accompanied by the Holy Spirit. By the Spirit He went through His earthly life victorious, even though He was as fully God as He was fully man, He faced temptations as a man and overcame. Paul in writing to the Philippians said, *Have this mind among yourselves, which is yours in Christ Jesus, who, though he was in the form of God, did not count equality with God a thing to be grasped, but emptied himself, taking the form of a servant, being born in the likeness of men. And being found in human form, he humbled himself, and became obedient unto death, even death on a cross* (Phil. 2: 5–8). Christ went through life completely dependent on God so as to be an example for us. As He overcame by the Spirit we too can overcome by the Spirit.

The power of the Holy Spirit is our greatest need. This power is available to each of us today. As the Spirit of God guided Jesus throughout His earthly life, He is available to guide us. Let us ask for the Spirit in our lives. Let us believe that by faith He will enter our lives. Let us claim Him as constant companion in our lives as we face the challenges that are before us.

Chapter Five
Come Holy Spirit

It was the day before Jesus was to be crucified. He had already eaten the last supper with the disciples. Knowing that His *hour had come to depart out of this world to the Father* (John 13:1), He said to His disciples, *Where I am going you cannot follow after me now; but you shall follow afterward* (John 13:36). The disciples were filled with sadness. Their hopes were dashed and their selfish ambitions seemed fruitless. Jesus told them that He was going away, but they were not to be left comfortless. Christ, in an attempt to renew hopes in the hearts of His disciples said, *And I will pray the Father, and he will give you another Counselor, to be with you for ever.* (John 14:16). It was the Holy Spirit who was to be the gift of the Father through His Son to the disciples. It was the Holy Spirit, the third member of the Godhead, who was to take over the role of Jesus on earth. It was the Holy Spirit who had been the companion of Jesus throughout His earthly ministry, who was now to make the teachings of Jesus plain to the disciples and to guide them as well as guide those who would come after them to the kingdom of God.

The Holy Spirit Coming In The Name Of The Son

Concerning the coming of the Holy Spirit, Jesus said, *These things I have spoken to you, while I am still with you. But the Counselor, the Holy Spirit, whom the Father will send in my name, he will teach you all things, and bring to your remembrance all that I have said to you.* (John 14:25, 26).

Christ said that *I have come in my Father's name* (John 5:43), and later He said, *I told you, and you do not believe. The* works that I do in my Father's name, they bear witness to me (John 10:25). Christ came in His Father's name and now He, the Holy Spirit, was sent by the Father in the name of the Son. As the Son came and operated in the name of the Father, so the Spirit was to come and operate in the name of the Son.

The Mission Of The Holy Spirit

In His discourse with His disciples, Jesus revealed the true mission of the Holy Spirit. He said, *And I will pray the Father and He will give you another Counselor, to be with you forever* (John 14:16). The greatest gift of Jesus to His disciples is the gift of the Holy Spirit. Our task now is not to pray that the Holy Spirit be sent to us, but to seek the Holy Spirit's cleansing. We need to confess and forsake our sins, to be cleansed by the blood of the Lamb, to have the Holy Spirit dwell in our hearts. Christ said, *Behold I stand at the door and knock, if anyone hears my voice and open the door, I will come into him and eat with him, and he with me* (Revelation. 3:20).

God desires to enter into each heart. He wants to live within us, for only then will we be able to gain victory over sin. We cannot overcome the devil by ourselves, we need the in-filling of the Spirit to withstand the fiery darts of the wicked one. Christ further taught that the Holy Spirit will *Teach you all things, and bring to your remembrance all that I have said to you* (John 14:26). The Saviour also said, *When the Spirit of truth comes, he will guide you into all the truth for he will not speak on his own authority, but whatever he hears, he will speak, and he will declare to you the things that are to come. He will glorify me for he will take what is mine and declare it to you* (John 16:13–14).

The Spirit's mission includes, abiding in the believer, empowering the church through indwelling its members, teaching the believers and bringing to remembrance the things that have been taught by God. This work is essential for those who are seeking regeneration in Christ. Ellen White said, "The Holy Spirit seeks to abide in each soul. If He is welcomed as an honored guest, those who receive Him will be made complete in Christ. The good work began will be finished; the holy thoughts, heavenly affections, and Christ-like actions will take the place of impure thoughts, perverse sentiments and rebellious acts." (*Counsel on Health*, 561).

The Holy Spirit also has a mission to the world. *And when he is come, he will convince the world concerning sin and righteousness and judgment: concerning sin, because they do not believe in me; concerning righteousness because I go to the Father, and you will see me no more; concerning judgment, because the ruler of this world is judged* (John 16:8–11).

The mission of the Spirit is in no way limited to the church. His work impacts every man and woman in this world. The Spirit of God is constantly wooing sinners to come to God. He shows the folly of staying in sin, He reveals the pitfalls and the consequences of sin. He shows the benefits of a regenerated life in Christ and the joy that salvation brings. Oh, that sinners would yield to the constant prompting of the Spirit, then surely we would see a better world, more reflective of the righteousness of Jesus Christ.

Disciples Unfitted For The Task

Leroy E. Froom, in his book, *Coming of the Comforter*, page 83, said "When Jesus was gathering the dozen men about him through whom he would found the Christian church, he did not seek them in the venerable schools of the rabbis, or in the exclusive circle of the Sanhedrin. He did not send to Greece, the center of philosophy and culture, for His disciples. Nor did he go to Rome, the home of legislative genius and military powers, to find His apostles. No, He trod the shining shores of Galilee, and selected humble men whose hearts were big enough to admit the Lord of Glory; men who would finally be willing to be nothing that Christ might be everything; men who through the Holy Spirit could work, unhampered by human sophistry, selfishness, or superiority."

These men of humble background were chosen by Jesus to be His closest buddies. They were to be prepared to carry out the work of Jesus Christ in the world. Their work was not only to impact the population alive then, but it was to resound through the centuries. But before Christ's death they were not ready to receive the full power of the Holy Spirit.

Even though Christ had spent three and a half years with them and never failed to instruct them in every way, they were not ready to go forth to the world and proclaim the good news of salvation. With all their privileges in associating so closely with the Master Teacher, with all the opportunities to witness His miracle working power, the disciples were still not ready to face the world with the gospel commission.

Their great desire was to have immediate honor and glory for themselves. They had not grasped the greatest vision of a finished work in Christ. They exclaimed, *But we had hoped that he was the one to redeem Israel* (Luke 24:21). Filled with delight at the resurrection of Jesus Christ they asked Him, *Lord will you at this time restore the kingdom of Israel?* (Acts 1:6).

The disciples were fixed on earthly things while Christ was trying to move them beyond the earthly horizon to see the wider mission of preparing the earth for the second coming. "They did not see that His death meant life to them. They did not understand that apparent defeat was the way to victory, and that darkness was the price of light." (*Coming of the Comforter*, 84).

Christ had spoken to His disciples of His death and resurrection. *And taking the twelve, he said to them, "Behold, we are going up to Jerusalem, and everything that is written of the Son of man by the prophets will be accomplished. For he will be delivered to the Gentiles, and will be mocked and shamefully treated and spit upon; they will scourge him and kill him, and on the third day he will rise." But they understood none of those things; this saying was hid from them, and they did not grasp what was said* (Luke 18: 31–34).

The disciples failed to acknowledge the life mission of Jesus. They had set their own path to travel, but Jesus did not leave them to their own wishes. He was constantly leading them to higher ground.

In view of the eminent departure of Jesus, the coming of the Holy Spirit was an advantage to the disciples. "Cumbered with humanity, Christ could not be in every place personally. Therefore, it was for their interest that He should go to the Father, and send the Spirit to be his successor on earth. No one could then have any advantage because of his location or his personal contact with Christ. By the Spirit the Saviour would be available to all. In this sense He would be nearer to them than if He had not ascended on high." (*Desire of Ages*, 669).

After the resurrection of Jesus, He went to His disciples and commissioned them *Go therefore and make disciples of all nations, baptizing them in the name of the Father, and of the Son and of the Holy Spirit, teaching them to observe all that I have commanded you; and lo, I am with you always, to the close of the age* (Matthew 28:19, 20).

This was the mission of the disciples on earth. It was for this task Jesus had called them from the side of the sea. Christ had said to them long before, *Follow me and I will make you fishers of men* (Matthew 4:19). They were to go and seek after the souls of mankind and lead them to the foot of the cross where they can experience the flowing stream of Calvary and be cleansed from sin by His own blood.

Leroy E. Froom said, "No one is equipped for gospel service unless and until endowed with this heavenly power. Knowledge is not enough; activity is not enough; one must have the power of the Holy Spirit." (*Coming of the Comforter*, 86)

Ellen White said, "What we need is the baptism of the Holy Spirit. Without this, we are no more fitted to be sent forth to the world than were the disciples after the crucifixion of their Lord. Jesus knew their destitution, and told them to tarry in Jerusalem until they should be endowed with power from on high." ("Review and Herald," February 18,

1890). "The preaching of the word will be of no avail without the continual presence and aid of the Holy Spirit. This is the only effectual teaching of divine truth. Only when the truth is accompanied to the heart by the Spirit, will it quicken the conscience or transform the life" (*Desire of Ages*, 671).

Luke said in the book of Acts, *And while staying with them he charged them not to depart from Jerusalem, but to wait for the promise of the Father, which, he said, "you heard from me, for John baptized with water, but before many days you shall be baptized with the Holy Spirit"* (Acts 1:4, 5).

The Promised outpouring of the Holy Spirit was to be the beginning of a new era in the Christian church. This was to be a fulfillment of the prophecies of the Old Testament. Some of the principal prophets who spoke of the coming of the Spirit are David, Psalm 68: 18; Solomon, Proverbs 1:23; Isaiah, Isaiah 32:15; Ezekiel, Ezekiel 36:28; and 39: 29; Joel, Joel 2:28 and Haggai, Haggai 2: 9. Just as John the Baptist announced the coming of the Lord, so Christ announced the coming of the Holy Spirit. That same Spirit that fell upon the disciples at Pentecost needs to fall upon each of us today.

Chapter Six

The Upper Room Experience

The disciples *returned to Jerusalem from the mount called Olivet; which is near Jerusalem, a sabbath day's journey away, and when they had entered, they went up to the upper room...All these with one accord devoted themselves to prayer together with the women and Mary the mother of Jesus, and with his brothers* (Acts 1: 12–14).

It is noteworthy that the women were assembled with the other disciples in the upper room. They, along with the men, were engaged in prayer waiting on the outpouring of the Holy Spirit. In God's eyes there is no gender gap as far as the receiving and working of the Holy Spirit is concerned. In fact Peter later said, *Truly I perceive that God shows no partiality, but in every nation anyone who fears him and does what is right is acceptable to him* (Acts 10: 34, 35).

Humble Men Were Chosen

These disciples were not the elite of the society, they were not the most educated in the schools of the Rabbis, nor were they members of the Sanhedrin. Their main qualification was that they obeyed the voice of Jesus and came to the upper room in Jerusalem. Something marvelous was about to happen. A new phase of the gospel was about to begin. God had selected his chosen vessels who were to carry out the most important task ever entrusted to mankind.

Those who followed Christ were the humble people, those who were seeking a better way, those who recognized Christ as the Messiah and Saviour of the race. Ellen White said, "Jesus chose unlearned fishermen because they had not

33

been schooled in the traditions and erroneous customs of their time. They were men of native abilities, and they were humble and teachable, men whom He could educate for His work." (*Desire of Ages*, 250).

The Disciples Waited For
The Power Promised By Jesus

In the upper room the disciples began to experience a change of attitude. They began to focus on their true mission. Peter led out in the selection of Matthias to succeed Judas who had betrayed his Lord. (Acts 1:22). They now realized that they needed to be ready for the outpouring of the Spirit. The promise of the Father was about to be fulfilled and each of them must avail himself to receive this power.

"As the disciples waited for the fulfillment of the promise, they humbled their hearts in true repentance and confessed their unbelief and prayed with intense earnestness for fitness to meet men in their daily intercourse, to speak words that would lead sinners to Christ. Putting away all differences, all desire for supremacy, they came close together in Christian fellowship. They drew nearer and nearer to God, as they did they realized what a privilege had been theirs in being permitted to associate so closely with Christ. Sadness filled their hearts as they thought of how many times they had grieved Him by their slowness of comprehension, their failure to understand the lessons that for their good that He was trying to teach them. These days of preparation were days of deep heart searching. The disciples felt their spiritual need and cried to the Lord for holy unction that was to fit them for the work of the salvation of souls. They realized that the gospel was to be carried to the whole world, and they claimed the power that Christ had promised" (*Acts of the Apostles*, 36, 37).

The nine days prior to the days of Pentecost was a time of preparation. Christ had declared that *All authority in heaven and on earth has been given to me* (Matthew 28:18). It was with that backdrop that He gave the disciples the great commission *to go and make disciples of all nations* (Matthew 28:19). For them to fulfill this great responsibility, they needed the power of the Holy Spirit. Thus Jesus promised them that, *you shall receive power when the Holy Spirit has come upon you; and you shall be my witnesses in Jerusalem and in all Judea and Samaria and to the end of the earth* (Acts 1:8)

The key word in the above text is *power*. Coming from the Greek word *dunamis* from which we derive dynamite, dynamic, and dynamo. We need this dynamite to blast away the deep sins that are lodged in our hearts. We need this dynamite to reorganize our selfish hearts and rearrange our focus. We need this *dunamis* to break down our adamant will of indifference, formalism and prejudice. It is only through this power that the earth will be filled with the glory of God so that the light of Christ's righteousness will shine in every *nook and cranny*.

It was a privilege to visit Victoria Falls in Zimbabwe, Africa. These falls are created by the Zambezi River that runs from Zambia into Zimbabwe. At the time I went to see these great falls, the river was at its strongest. This created a mighty cascade that fell hundreds of feet from the Zambian side of the river to the Zimbabwean side. What an awesome sight that was. It was greater than what I saw on the Canadian side of the Niagara Falls. Millions of kilowatts of electricity are generated from these falls. The power generated supplies millions of people with adequate electricity for domestic and commercial use.

What took place at Pentecost was far greater than the power of Victoria and Niagara Falls combined. The power manifested at Pentecost cannot be measured by human instruments. This was Divine power that started the greatest movement that ever took place in human history. "As the Divine endowment...the power of the Holy Spirit...was given to the disciples, so it will today be given to all who seek aright. This power alone is able to make us wise unto salvation and to fit us for courts above" (*Testimonies*, vol. 7. 273).

Power to Witness

The purpose for which the Holy Spirit power was given to the disciples was to witness. Christ said, *And ye shall be my witnesses* (Acts 1:8). Those who seek for the power of the Spirit must also be prepared to go and tell the story of Jesus Christ. The Holy Spirit is not given for one to sit and do nothing. He is not given only for one to sit down in church and enjoy the fellowship of the saints and the benefits of the body of Christ. No, those who are empowered by the Spirit have a sacred responsibility of proclaiming the gospel for Christ to others, by the life we live and the words we speak and the things we do. Everyone might not be able to preach like Peter or Paul, everyone might not be able to sing like angels, but everyone can do something to share the love of Jesus with others.

In the letter written by Ellen White to Mrs. Harper, September 23, 1894, she said, "Every truly concerted soul will be intensely desirous to bring others from the darkness of error into the marvelous light of the righteousness of Jesus Christ. The great outpouring of the Spirit of God which lightens the whole earth with His glory will not come until we have an enlightened people who know by experience what it means to be laborers together with God. God cannot pour out His Spirit when selfishness and self indulgences are so manifested, when a spirit prevails that if put into words would express the answer of Cain.—am I my brother's keeper?" (Letter 31, 1894, 11).

To be a witness we must know something. To be a witness for Christ, we must know Christ. No one can be a credible witness who has not seen or experienced the event. One can be charged for perjury if one goes into a courtroom and bear witness to what one has not seen or experienced. The witness must know the facts, not *hear say*, but the facts, and truthfully declare them.

To be a witness for Christ requires a personal experience with Christ. David said, *O taste and see that the Lord is good!* (Psalms 34:8). Those who drink from the fountain of salvation can surely tell others of the goodness of God. Like the woman at the well, when we taste of the water of life, we will be desirous of sharing the good news with those we love and care for, those who are in need of the Saviour. *The woman left her water jar and went away into the city, and said to the people, "Come, see a man who told me all that I ever did. Can this be the Christ?" They went out of the city and were coming to him* (John 4: 28–30).

The English word, *witness* comes from the Anglo-Saxon word *witam* meaning "I know." The reason for such little witnessing among us is that we do not really know Jesus Christ. If you know Him, you will tell others about Him. How can we witness if we have nothing to witness to.

We can know Jesus Christ by seeking after Him. We can know Jesus Christ by studying His word. We can know Jesus Christ by praying and entering into conversation with Him. We can speak to Him and listen to Him speak back to us. An experiential knowledge of Jesus Christ is essential if we are to be witnesses of Christ. May this be our experience.

Days of Waiting

There were ten days between the ascension of Jesus and the day of Pentecost. As earlier mentioned, these ten days were days of preparation for the outpouring of the Holy Spirit. The disciples went through moments of great agony wherein they were engaged in deep heart searching. They wanted to be sure that they were ready for the outpouring of the Spirit.

Wesley Amundsen in his book *The Power of Pentecost* outlined the steps taken by the disciples during these ten days of waiting for the outpouring of the Holy Spirit. These are worthy of note. They are humility, confessions, heart preparation, unity, self abrogation, fellowship of the believers, compassion, soul hunger for righteousness, passion for souls and finally, they were in one accord.

Ellen White said, "Putting away all differences; the disciples prepared for the promised power. It took real effort for the disciples to gather the courage to confess their faults to one another. These words are an assurance that a unity of spirit was achieved: every Christian saw in his brother the divine similitude of love benevolence. Instead of seeing one another's weaknesses, faults, and errors they saw each other as loving, kind, and filled with a Christ-centered unity. One in interest prevailed" (*Testimonies to the Churches*. Vol. 8, 20).

In the upper room, the Spirit of God pierced their hearts. For the first time they understood fully what Christ meant when He requested in prayer to His father, *that they may all be one; even as thou, Father, art in me, and I in thee, that they also may be in us, so that the world may believe that thou hast sent me* (John 17:21).

For these ten days, the disciples came closer to each other and subsequently closer to God. They developed the virtue of righteousness that would fit them to represent Christ in the world, all one hundred and twenty of them in the upper room, united and prayed for the outpouring which was to be sent to them in answer to prayer. The Saviour had prayed for them. Now they were to pray for each other and make supplication to their heavenly Father, through Jesus Christ. The Holy Spirit wanted to come to them, the time was just about fulfilled and they were just about ready to tap into the sources of supernatural power.

"When the church awakes to the sense of her holy calling, many more fervent and effective prayers will ascend to heaven for the Holy Spirit to point out the work and duty of God's people regarding the salvation of souls. We have the standing promise that God will draw near to every seeking soul ... when the church awakes to a sense of what must be done in our world, the members will have travail of souls for those who know not God and who in their spiritual ignorance cannot understand the truth for this time" (*Selected Messages*, Book One 116).

The disciples not only had a personal experience with God during those ten days of preparation, but they developed a passion for souls like they had never had before. Now the desires of selfish ambitions were completely removed from them, they could only see others and what they could do to help save the lost.

The disciples pressed their petitions even to the throne room of God. They remembered the words of the Master, *Truly, truly, I say to you, if you ask anything of the Father, he will give it to you in my name* (John 16:23). They were now ready to claim the promise of Jesus for themselves, for now they had come in oneness with Jesus Christ. Pentecost, so long awaited, was now about to be theirs. Even though the multitude gathered in the city had no knowledge of what was going on in the upper room, the one hundred and twenty disciples were ready for the greatest outpouring of the Holy Spirit the world has ever known. It was on the verge of happening. The disciples were ready and God was ready to pour out His Spirit upon them.

Chapter Seven

The Day of Pentecost

Pentecost Defined

As we examine what transpired on the day of Pentecost, it might be helpful for us to briefly look at the history of the Feast of Pentecost.

Pentecost is defined as the Festival of Wheat Harvest or the First Fruits of Wheat Harvest, (Exodus 34:22). In the time of the Old Testament, Pentecost was one of the three annual festivals that all Hebrew men were required to attend (Leviticus 23:37). It was a day festival, a ceremonial Sabbath, where two loaves of fine flour baked with leaven, together with oatmeal sacrifices, were offered to the Lord, (Leviticus 23: 17–21).

The term "Pentecost" refers to the fiftieth day after Passover. Pentecost is also celebrated as a commemoration of the giving of the Law on Mount Sinai. Christ's death coincided with the Passover, He was the Pascal Lamb who died for the sins of the world. It was He that all previous Passover ceremonies were pointing to. And now He presented Himself as the true lamb, undefiled and untainted with the sins of this world. Jesus took the place of the innocent lamb the priest would kill on the altar, on the behalf of the sins of the people.

The ascension of our Lord was forty days after the Passover and it was ten days later that the Pentecostal feast was celebrated. It was those ten days the disciples spent in the upper room in preparation for the outpouring of the Holy Spirit. Pentecost was to signal a new day, a new era in the lives of the disciples that inaugurated the Christian Era.

The Outpouring

When the day of Pentecost had come, they were all together in one place. And suddenly a sound came from heaven like the rush of a mighty wind, and it filled the house where they were sitting. And there appeared to then tongues as of fire, distributed and resting on each one of them. And they were all filled with the Holy Spirit and began to speak in other tongues, as the Spirit gave them utterance (Acts 2:1–4).

After ten days of praying, rejoicing and blessing God, the disciples came into one accord thus making room for the outpouring of the Comforter. This was the promise that Christ made to them. *Nevertheless I tell you the truth: it is to your advantage that I go away, for if I do not go away the Counselor will not come to you; But if I go, I will send him to you* (John 16:7).

As the Spirit came upon the waiting disciples, He did not come like an unexpected guest, He did not come secretly, quietly tip toeing into the hall where they assembled. No! He came *like the rush of a mighty wind, and it filled all the house where they were sitting* (Acts 2:2). As the Holy Spirit descended, *there appeared to them tongues as of fire, distributed and resting on each one of them. And they were all filled with the Holy Spirit and began to speak in other tongues, as the Spirit gave them utterance* (Acts 2:3, 4).

Ellen White said, "Christ's ascension to heaven was the signal that His followers were to receive the promised blessing. For this they were to wait before they entered their work. When Christ passed within the heavenly gates, He was enthroned amongst the adoration of the angels. As soon as this ceremony was completed, the Holy Spirit descended upon the disciples in rich currents, and Christ was indeed glorified, even with the glory He had with the Father from all eternity. Pentecostal outpouring was heaven's communication that the Redeemer's inauguration was accomplished. According to His promise He had sent the Holy Spirit from heaven to His followers as a token that He had, as priest and king, received all authority in heaven and on earth, and was the anointed one over His people" (*Acts of the Apostles*, 38, 39).

The Holy Spirit came in the form of tongues to give the unlearned disciples the ability to communicate to the world, the gospel of Jesus Christ in different languages. Assembled there in Jerusalem was a microcosm of the world. There were people from several countries. Outside of the upper room the gift of languages gave the disciple an immediate opportunity to bear witness of the love of God. *Now there were dwelling in Jerusalem Jews, devout men from every nation under the heaven. And at this sound, the multitude came together and they were bewildered, because each one heard them speaking in their own language* (Acts 2: 5, 6).

What a great phenomenon! The gift of languages gave new dimension to the disciples ability to communicate the gospel of Jesus Christ. They were equipped to take the gospel to the world. God's remnant church today is carrying the gospel to the whole world and thousands are rushing to Jesus to be saved.

The Holy Spirit came "as of fire." This symbol of fire was to indicate to the disciples that the movement of the Spirit was not a lifeless, cold experience, but one that is characterized with energy. The gospel of Christ is substantial enough to ignite energy into the lives of the believers. The gospel of Christ presented with great passion gives life, life to those who are dead in trespasses and sin, life to the lifeless bodies that have been wounded by the adversary, life to those who are committed to bear the gift of righteousness.

At Pentecost the Holy Spirit came as a gift from God. The disciples had no claim to this gift. He did not come simply because the disciples prayed. He came as a promise of the Father through the Son to these waiting disciples. The Holy Spirit was not limited to those at Pentecost, but is also a gift to all who accept Christ as Lord of their lives. He even works on the hearts of those who know not God to lead them to repentance. *And when he comes, he will convince the world concerning sin and righteousness and judgment* (John 16:8).

The outpouring of the Spirit brought new dimension to the disciples abilities to proclaim the gospel of Jesus Christ. G. Campbell Morgan said, "The coming of the Holy Spirit was the dawn of the brightest day the world had seen since the fall" (*Understanding the Holy Spirit*, 87).

These one hundred and twenty disciples were not only refreshed, they were empowered for the great task that was before them. They accepted the gift of the Holy Spirit and went forth with boldness in proclaiming the risen Saviour and the need to repent and come to Him for salvation. Never before were they so equipped, never before did they understand the purposes for which they were called. Now they had a clear vision of their mission on earth. The disciples who had spent three and a half years at the Saviour's feet did not learn all the lessons He taught them. Jesus could not entrust the message to the world to them without the accompanying presence of the Holy Spirit. The Saviour could not depend on their human abilities to accomplish the awesome task of presenting the gospel message to the world. So the gift of the Holy Spirit was most essential in preparing and enabling the disciples to fulfill their mission.

Ellen White said, "The Saviour knew that no argument, however logical, would melt hard hearts or break through the crust of worldliness and selfishness. He knew that His disciples must receive the heavenly endowment so that the gospel would be effective when it was proclaimed. Hearts are made warm and lips made eloquent when accented by a living knowledge of Him who is the way, the truth and the life. The work committed to the disciples would require great efficiency; for the tide of evil ran strong against them. A vigilant, determined leader was in command of the fortress of darkness, and the followers of Christ could battle for the right only through the help that God, by His Spirit, would give them" (*Acts of the Apostles*, 37).

Satan lost the battle at Calvary and further lost on Sunday at the resurrection. He was determined to sabotage the presentation of the gospel of Christ, but now his plans were thwarted. The Holy Spirit had come and the disciples had received His power. They were not the same selfish, self-seeking, jealous disciples anymore. They were now agents in the hand of God who were willing to be used by God. The stage was now set for the commencement of a new era and there were people waiting on the outside of the upper room to hear them.

Chapter Eight

Result of Pentecost

Filled with the Holy Ghost, the disciples turned to the amazed crowd where they were gathered. There were people who had come to the feast of Pentecost from many nations. Assembled at Jerusalem were the Parthians, Medes, Elamites and residents of Mesopotamia, Judea and Cappodocia, Pontius and Asia, Phrygia and Pamphylia, Egypt and the parts of Libya belonging to Cyrene, and visitors from Rome, both Jews and proselytes, Cratons and Arabians (Acts 2: 9–12).

The multitude which was assembled heard the gospel of Christ proclaimed in their *own language, and they were amazed and wondered, saying, "are not all those who speak Galileans? And how is it that we hear each of us in his own native language?"* (Acts 2: 7, 8). There was understandably amazement at this phenomenal manifestation. Obviously, the priests and rabbis of the people were confounded by the manifestation of Holy Ghost power. The Jewish leaders said, *"they were filled with new wine," while others asked each other, "What does this mean?"* (Acts 2:13).

Peter, being overcome by the power of the Holy Spirit, with the other disciples, began to preach to the multitude. They explained that they were not drunk, but that what they were seeing was spoken of by the prophet Joel who declared, *And it shall come to pass afterward, that I will pour out my Spirit upon all flesh; your sons and your daughters shall prophesy, your old men shall dream dreams and your young men shall see visions. Even upon menservants and maidservants in those days, I will pour out my Spirit* (Joel 2: 28, 29).

Peter spoke about the death and resurrection of Jesus Christ. How Jesus came to save the lost. How He was crucified and killed by "lawless men." Peter continued by saying that Jesus was raised from the dead as David had written, *I saw the Lord always before me, for he is at my right hand that I may not be shaken; therefore my heart was glad, and my tongue rejoiced; moreover my flesh will dwell in hope, for thou wilt not abandon my soul to Hades, nor let the Holy One see corruption* (Acts 2: 25–27).

In an attempt to convince his hearers, who were basically Jews, Peter quoted from the patriarch David, whom the Jews cherished as a prophet. Peter established in the minds of his hearers that what was taking place was authentic and had prophetic bearing. Peter lifted up the message of the prophet Joel to them as he cited the prophecy, *And it shall come to pass afterward, that I will pour out my Spirit on all flesh; your sons and your daughters shall prophecy, your old men shall dream dreams, and your young men shall see visions. Even upon the menservants and maidservants in those days, I will pour out my Spirit* (Joel 2:28,29).

The sermon Peter preached went to the heart of the matter. Those who had condemned Jesus to death were in the audience and Peter, knowing that, did not spare them in speaking of Jesus. Peter emphasized how Jesus was unjustly killed. *This Jesus God raised up, and of that we all are witnesses. Being therefore exalted at the right hand of God, and having received from the Father the promise of the Holy Spirit, he has poured out this which you see and hear* (Acts 2:32,33).

The message of Peter undoubtedly had a great impact on his listeners for Luke says, *Now when they heard this, they were cut to the heart, and said to Peter and the rest of the apostles, 'Brethren, what shall we do?' And Peter said to them, 'Repent, and be baptized every one of you in the name of Jesus Christ for the forgiveness of your sins; and you shall receive the gift of the Holy Spirit. For the promise is to you and to your children and to all that are far off, every one whom the Lord our God calls to Him'* (Acts 2:37–39). The message stirred their consciences which resulted in a great harvest of souls.

So those who received his word were baptized, and there were added that day about three thousand souls (Acts 2:41).

In Jerusalem, the stronghold of Judaism, filled with representatives from every side; in Jerusalem where Christ, fifty days earlier was condemned to die by those whom He came to save; in Jerusalem, where He had been scoffed at, and ridiculed—there were added to the church in one day some three thousand souls.

This was an immense harvest of souls, and what a joy that the apostles did not take the credit for themselves. "They did not regard this wonderful ingathering as a result of their own efforts; they realized that they were entering other men's labors. Ever since the fall of Adam, Christ had been committing to chosen servants the seed of His Word to be sown in human hearts. During His life on this earth, He had sown the seed of truth and had watered it with His blood. The conversions that took place on the Day of Pentecost were the result of this sowing, the harvest of Christ's work, revealing the power of His teaching" (*Acts of the Apostles*, 45).

"The arguments of the apostles alone, though clear and convincing, would not have removed the prejudice that had withstood so much evidence. But the Holy Spirit sent the arguments home to hearts with divine power. The words of the apostles were as sharp arrows of the Almighty, convicting men of their terrible guilt in rejecting and crucifying the Lord of glory" (*Ibid*, 45).

Weeks before the Pentecostal experience, the Apostles were discouraged, despondent, and feared for their very lives. Now at Pentecost, they were revitalized, regenerated, mission-focused, and filled with boldness. As they spoke to that huge audience, they had no fear of reprisal. Their only desire was to exalt Christ Whom they had forsaken.

Their efforts were immediately rewarded, for a great multitude gave assent to the gospel of Jesus Christ and were baptized on the first day of the new era. Their faith in God was put to the test and was immediately rewarded. As the days and weeks went by, many more were added to the church. *And day by day, attending the temple together and breaking bread in their homes, they partook of food with glad and generous hearts, praising God and having favor with all the people. And the Lord added to their number day by day those who were being saved* (Acts 2:46,47).

Pentecost brought the church together in "one accord", "one heart and soul" (Acts 2:46). The disciples were united in their purpose of proclaiming the gospel and fulfilling the commission of Jesus Christ. Nothing is so powerful as people coming together for one common cause. Tyrants have crumbled because people rallied together. Nations have changed their courses because people came together. The devils fear and tremble when God's people come together. There is power in unity. With unity we can put the Devil on notice. With unity there can be the greatest revival and reformation we have ever seen. For this unity, we must strive. With broken and contrite hearts, we must come before God, seeking a oneness that will empower us for the divine task that God has for us.

"To us today, as surely as with the first disciples, the promise of the Spirit belongs. God will today endow men and women with power from above, as He endowed those who, on the day of Pentecost, heard the word of salvation. At this very hour, His Spirit and His grace are for all who need them and will take Him at His word" (*Testimonies to the Church*, vol. 8, 20). Pentecost brought springtime to the church again. That which seemed to be dying was alive again. Christ was resurrected and ascended to glory, and the disciples were recharged with divine energy to spread the good news of salvation that is only in Christ.

Ellen White, in describing the events in the proclamation of the gospel in the last days said, "The great work of the gospel is not to close with less manifestation of the power of God than marked its opening. The prophecies which were fulfilled in the outpouring of the former rain at the opening of the gospel, are again to be fulfilled in the latter rain at its close. Here are 'the times of refreshing' to which the apostle Peter looked forward when he said, 'Repent ye therefore, and be converted, that your sins may be blotted out when the times of refreshing shall come from the presence of the Lord; and He shall send Jesus' (Acts 3:19, 20).

Servants of God, with their faces lighted up and shining with holy consecration, will hasten from place to place to proclaim the message from heaven. By thousands of voices, all over the earth, the warning will be given. Miracles will be wrought, the sick will be healed, and signs and wonders will follow the believers. Satan also works with lying wonders, even bringing down fire from heaven in the sight of men. Thus the inhabitants of the earth will be brought to take their stand.

The message will be carried not so much by argument as by the deep conviction of the Spirit of God. The arguments have been presented. The seed has been sown, and now it will spring up and bear fruit" (*The Great Controversy*, 611,612).

The Spirit of God is at work in the earth. There are thousands who are being converted and finding a resting place in Christ. But greater work is still ahead of us, and this cannot be fully accomplished without our making ourselves available, like the apostles, to God, for the in-filling of the Holy Spirit.

Even though some work is being done, there is a greater work to be done. Millions are going down in Christless graves. There are still millions who have not had a chance to hear the good news of salvation. Now is the time for us to avail ourselves of the divine power to accomplish the task of evangelizing the world.

Each one must have his or her own experience with the Lord. Each one must be emptied of self and anything that will hinder the in-filling of the Holy Spirit. The church consists of individuals, and if the church is languishing, then its members are languishing. Today there needs to be a renewal of primitive godliness in the church of God. There needs to be a refreshing of the Spirit of God in the life of the church. As it was after Pentecost, so can it be now. There was oneness among the members; there was singleness of heart.

With this focus, much was accomplished. Let us today go back and reclaim the spirit of the disciples after Pentecost.

Chapter Nine

The Holy Spirit and the Church

The Church Defined

In these last days God has chosen a people to be His standard bearers to the world. We call these people "The Church." The word "church" comes from the Greek word *ecclesia* which means "called out." God has called out a people from the world to represent Him in these times. Peter refers to them as *a chosen race, a royal priesthood, a holy nation, God's own people, that ye may declare the wonderful deeds of Him who called you out of darkness into His marvelous light* (I Peter 2:9).

The Church is subject to Christ, and the Holy Spirit is given to bring the Church into oneness with Christ, its Head. The Church cannot survive independent of Christ. It cannot survive independent of the Holy Spirit because it is the Holy Spirit that will perfect the Church to meet Christ on His return for her whom He has called His "bride."

The Body of Christ

The Church is the body of Christ. *Now ye are the body of Christ and individually members of it* (I Corinthians 12:27). The Church is not just an organization with a structure and attractive buildings. In fact, that is not the Church at all. Those who constitute the Church are those who have accepted Christ as their Lord and Saviour, those who have been washed in His blood and have their names written in the Lamb's Book of Life.

There are some who have their names chronicled in a church's registry and believe that this will ensure them a place in heaven, but nothing is farther from the truth. God's true church is made up of those whom He has called and who have responded to His invitation and who are resting in His arms; those who have been *born of water and the Spirit* (John 3:1–5).

Each member of the Body of Christ is called and incorporated into the body by the Holy Spirit. No other power can add to or take away from the Church. Men may add to organizations, but this does not make one a member of the Church of God. For one to become a member of the divine church, one must come through Jesus Christ who is *the way, the truth and the life* (John 14:6).

The Holy Spirit Gives Life to the Church

Unfortunately, there are churches that are as dry as the Hills of Gilboa and cold as the Arctic. This environment presents a bad picture of what the Church is and why the Church is in existence. The Church that Jesus left was on fire for Him, a fire burning in the hearts of men and women, a fire refining souls and bringing them into harmony with Christ. This fire was kindled at Pentecost and it has been burning through the ages. It is still burning even now. It is sad, however, that there are some who have not been ignited by the flames of the Holy Spirit, but they continue in their dryness and insipid atmosphere.

It is the Spirit that gives life to the Church. And it is also the Spirit that sustains that life in the Church. Paul said, *For by one Spirit we were all baptized into one body—Jews or Greeks, slave or free, and all were made to drink of one Spirit* (I Corinthians 12:13).

The Holy Spirit is a key element of our new life. It is He that energizes us in our daily walk with God. It is He that renews our spirits every day. It is He that defends us as we fight the enemy of our souls. It is He that quickens our dead bodies of sin and gives us the new life of Christ's righteousness.

If the Spirit of him who raised Jesus from the dead dwells in you, he who raised Christ Jesus from the dead will give life to your mortal bodies also through his Spirit which dwells in you (Romans 8:11).

The woman of Samaria whom Christ met at Jacob's well was thirsty for salvation. Christ, the source of the water of life, met her at the well in the heat of the day. After entering into conversation with Jesus and hearing Him tell her all things concerning herself, she marveled. Jesus promised her if she would ask Him, He would give her "living water." He said, *Everyone who drinks of this water will thirst again, but whosoever drinks of the water that I shall give him will never thirst; the water that I give him will become in him a spring of water welling up to eternal life* (John 4:13,14).

Through the Spirit of God, a fountain is promised from which all sinners may drink so that the life of sin may die and the life of righteousness may live, even unto eternal life. It was on the Mount of Blessing, as Jesus taught His disciples, that He said, *Blessed are those who hunger and thirst for righteousness, for they shall be satisfied* (Matthew 5:6). A. B. Simpson said, "He has to make us so hungry and thirsty that we will fly to Him for His life and love. He has to press us into hard emergency so as to constrain us to receive His fullness. And thus He is watering, nourishing, filling and perfecting His glorious workmanship, and preparing it for the maturity of the Body and the fullness of Christ" (*The Holy Spirit*, 419).

The Holy Spirit Unites the Church

It is the Holy Spirit that unites the body of Christ. The physical body cannot stand up only with its bones; it needs the sinews and the muscles to keep it together and give it strength. So the body of Christ needs the Holy Spirit to keep its members, with their different identities and personalities, together for the purpose of ministry. Paul said, *For just as the body is one and has many members, and all the members of the body, though many, are one body, so it is with Christ* (I Corinthians 12:12).

On the day of Pentecost, as the disciples awaited the Holy Spirit, there was a sense of unity among them. *And when the day of Pentecost was fully come, they were all with one accord in one place* (Acts 2:1, KJV). For the disciples to be effective in carrying out the mission that was given them, they needed to come to oneness. This oneness resulted in the outpouring of the Spirit's power upon them. Because of that outpouring they were extremely effective.

The Holy Spirit unites us to Christ and to one another. One of Christ's last prayers to His Father was a prayer for unity. *And now I am no more in the world, but they are in the world, and I am coming to thee. Holy Father, keep them in thy name, which thou hast given me, that they may be one, even as we are one* (John 17:11). Later in the same chapter of John, as Christ continues in prayer, He said, *I do not pray for these only, but also for those who believe in me through their word, that they may all be one; even as thou, Father, art in me, and I in thee, that they also may be in us, so that the world may believe that thou hast sent me* (John 17:20,21).

For the Church to receive power to carry out the commission of the Lord Jesus Christ, the members must be in unity with each other and with God. We are weakened when strife and discord exist in our midst. There is a great work to be accomplished and every ounce of energy is needed to focus on the divine mission we have from God.

Ellen White said, "Let all dissension and strife cease. Let love and unity prevail. Let all move under the guidance of the Holy Spirit. If God's people will give themselves wholly to Him, He will restore to them the power they have lost by division. May God help us all to realize that disunion is weakness and that union is strength" (*Selected Messages*, Vol. 1, 85).

"When Christ's prayer is fully believed, when its instruction is brought into the daily life of God's people, unity of action will be seen in our ranks. Brother will be bound to brother by the golden bonds of love of Christ. The Spirit of God alone can bring about this oneness. He who sanctified Himself can sanctify His disciples. United with Him, they will be united with one another in the most holy faith. When we strive for this unity as God desires us to strive for it, it will come to us" (*Testimony To The Church,* vol. 8, 243).

The Holy Spirit Equipping the Church

On the day of Pentecost the disciples were given the gift of speaking foreign languages which they had never spoken. Most of those who came to Christ while He was on earth were humble, unlearned men and women who were to represent Christ to the then-known world. It would have been impossible for them to carry out this task without some miracle from God; and at the time of the visitation of the Spirit, one of the great phenomena was that the disciples spoke in other tongues. *And they were all filled with the Holy Spirit and began to speak in other tongues, as the Spirit gave them utterance* (Acts 2:4).

This gift of tongues gave the apostles the ability to be international evangelists, the gospel was not to be confined to Jerusalem and the regions round about, but *this gospel of the Kingdom will be preached throughout the whole world, as a testimony to all nations, and then the end will come* (Matthew 24; 14). The disciples were encouraged by this gift to communicate the gospel of their Lord and Master effectively with whomever they came in contact. Each time the gift was manifested, they had the assurance that the Lord was with them in their mission.

The Church received several other gifts from the Spirit to fulfill its mission. Paul said, *Concerning spiritual gifts, brethren, I do not want you to be uninformed. Now, there are varieties of gifts, but the same Spirit; and there are varieties of services, but the same Lord; and there are varieties of workings, but it is the same God who inspires them all in every one. To one is given, through the Spirit, the utterance of wisdom, and to another the utterance of knowledge, according to the same Spirit. To another faith, by the same Spirit, to another the gift of healing, by the same spirit, to another the working of miracles, to another prophecy, to another the ability to distinguish between spirits, to* another various kind of tongues. All these are inspired by the Spirit, who apportions to each one individually as he wills" (I Corinthians 12:1, 4–6, 8–11).

The gifts were given for the building up of the body of Christ and the perfecting of the saints. *And his gifts were that some should be apostles, some prophets, some evangelists, some pastors and teachers, to equip the saints for the work of ministry, for building up the body of Christ, until we all attain to unity of the faith and knowledge of the Son of God, to mature manhood, to the measure of the stature of the fullness of Christ* (Ephesians 4:11–13). There is no need for the Church to be in want. The Lord, through His Spirit, has supplied the Church with the necessary tools to perform its task. Like a symphony orchestra, the Church has the different instruments needed to play a melodious harmony so that it will be pleasing in the sight of heaven, and souls drifting in the tide of sin can find rescue in the arms of Jesus.

The Holy Spirit is
The Source of Power for the Church

In Christ's promise to His disciples He said, *But you shall receive power when the Holy Spirit has come upon you; and you shall be my witnesses in Jerusalem and in all Judea and Samaria, and to the ends of the earth"* (Acts 1:8). The church in apostolic days needed power to witness. They needed power to break down the walls of prejudice. God has promised to give this power which will change the minds of people.

There are several Greek words for power. One is *kretos* which implies physical strength. Another word is *exousia* which implies a ruler's authority. This was the same word used by Christ in giving the commission to His disciples when He said, *All authority in heaven and on earth has been given to me* (Matthew 28:18). In the book of Acts chapter 1, verse 8, the word used for power is *dunamis*. This word implies explosive energy and the continual steady power of the dynamo. The disciples needed this added dimension to do the extraordinary job that was assigned to them. They tapped into the source of Divine power to fulfill their task.

"The Holy Spirit is the source of power for the Church. He is the source of spiritual power for the individual Christian and the source of successful ministry by the Church as a collective enterprise. The power that attended the coming of the Holy Spirit at Pentecost is the same power we need today. The same Spirit awaits our demand and reception" (*Christ's Object Lessons*, 121).

Even though there is such a rich resource of power, the Church today is desperately lacking that power. Like the Laodcean Church, the remnant Church sometimes boasts that it has riches and in need of nothing. John, in recording the words of the angel said, *I know your works: you are neither cold nor hot. Would that you were cold or hot! So because you are lukewarm, and neither cold nor hot, I will spew you out of my mouth. For you say, I am rich and have prospered and I need nothing; not knowing that you are wretched, pitiable, poor, blind and naked* (Revelation 3:15–17).

This lukewarmness in the Church of Laodcea resulted in God saying that he was about to spew them out of His mouth (Revelation 3:16). What a terrible feeling it must be to be vomited out of the mouth of God! If there is anyone who could reach out to rescue us, it is God; yet due to the nauseating, complacent, self-satisfied nature of the Laodcean Christians, God could not digest them, but spewed them out of His mouth.

The story does not stop there, however. Through the mercies of God, He encouraged us to *buy from me gold refined by fire, that you may be rich, and white garments to clothe you and to keep the shame of your nakedness from being seen, and salve to anoint your eyes, that you may see* (Revelation 3:18).

"The Church is up-to-date. She has a wonderful organization. She has a marvelous machinery. The wheels are adjusted properly. But she lacks power. In spite of all our facilities, we do not have the power of conversion which should mark the remnant church. We are faltering in the conflict with worldliness, unbelief, and unrighteousness. While the Church is evangelizing the world, the world is secularizing the Church. Thus her efforts are neutralized. To attract and interest people, ministers are resorting to worldly methods that are miserable makeshifts for the power from on high. It is humiliating to think of some of these worldly experiments used—and so unnecessarily" (*Coming of the Comforter*, 131).

There is need for a revival and some are turning to that which made the apostolic church successful. There is a need for renewed power that will electrify the Church to meet its task. Not a false electricity, but one that originates in the Kingdom of God. There is a great work to be done and the power is available to go and do it. We must empty ourselves of those things that shut out the Spirit from our lives and let Him come in.

Leroy Froom asked, "Why so little fruit from so great an army? Ah, our relation to the Holy Spirit is too largely unrecognized and this is in His dispensation. Where are the men filled with the Holy Spirit as were men in the apostolic days? We are in greatest peril of depending on men, methods and money, instead of on Him who alone can raise up men, direct and vitalize them, equip them with right methods and release and bless the money needed" (*Coming of the Comforter*, 132).

In June, 1905, Ellen White wrote in the journal, Review and Herald, "As we survey the work of God today, we discern many needs. We need more workers, we need more money, we need buildings, we need equipment. But the greatest need of all is the need of sincere power. This power is available only through the Spirit of the living God."

As it was back then, so it is today. We cannot accomplish anything meaningful without the Holy Spirit's power. We may have the greatest plans, we may have the most modern technology, we may have all the financial resources needed, but without the power that was with the apostles at Pentecost, there will be no true gain. Let us ask for this power, let us believe God and His promise of the Spirit, and let us claim the promise in our lives and do the will of God.

Chapter Ten

The Baptism of the Holy Spirit

The subject of the baptism of the Spirit has been widely discussed and many have misunderstood it. The Scripture has been clear in its teachings, but so as to fit their theological opinions, many have diluted this subject.

Let us look at several scriptural passages to see how they address the subject of the baptism of the Holy Spirit. In the book of Matthew chapter three and verse eleven, John the Baptist was in the wilderness baptizing those who responded to his invitation to come to repentance. When the Pharisees and Sadducees also came, John said to them, *I baptize you with water for repentance, but he who is coming after me is mightier than I, whose sandals I am not worthy to carry; he will baptize you with the Holy Spirit and with fire* (Matthew 3:11).

The Gospel of Mark records, *I have baptized you with water; but he will baptize you with the Holy Spirit* (Mark 1:8). In the book of Luke, John is quoted as saying, *I baptize you with water; but he who is mightier than I is coming, the thong of whose sandals I am not worthy to untie; he will baptize you with the Holy Spirit and with fire* (Luke 3:16). John, the apostle of Jesus, also recorded the saying of John the Baptist. *I myself did not know him; but he who sent me to baptize with water said to me, "he on whom you see the Spirit descend and remain, this is he who baptizes with the Holy Spirit"* (John 1:33).

Luke recorded the words of Jesus: *For John baptized with water, but before many days you shall be baptized with the Holy Spirit* (Acts 1:5). Peter, in defense of his preaching to the Gentiles, before Jewish Christians in Jerusalem said,

And I remembered the word of the Lord, how he said, "John baptized with water, but you shall be baptized with the Holy Spirit" (Acts 11:16).

What is the Baptism of the Holy Spirit?

The word "baptism" comes from the Greek word *baptizo*, which means "to immerse", and it carries with it the idea of death and resurrection. When one is baptized by the Holy Spirit, one is dead to sin and raised to walk in newness of life.

Jesus was sinless, yet, so that He would set for us an example, went down into Jordan and was baptized by John. Thus He demonstrated to us that in the process of a renewal of life, we too must enter the water of baptism, immersed as He was immersed and be raised to a new life in Christ. *Therefore, if anyone is in Christ he is a new creation; the old has passed away, behold, the new has come* (II Corinthians 5:17).

At the baptism of Jesus Christ, *the heavens were opened, and he saw the Spirit of God descending like a dove and alighted on him* (Matthew 3:16). The Holy Spirit shared in this all-important event as Christ commenced His public ministry. The child of God who comes to Christ and is baptized must also experience the Spirit's blessings. For we are not only baptized into Christ, but also in the Spirit and the Father. We enter a relationship with the heavenly Trio that must never be broken.

In our search to find the answer to the question, "What is the baptism of the Holy Spirit?" we may find some answers in Christ's response to Nicodemus. *Jesus answered him, "Truly, truly I say to you, unless one is born anew, he cannot see the Kingdom of God." Nicodemus said to him, "How can a man be born when he is old? Can he enter the second time into his mother's womb and be born?" Jesus answered, "Truly, truly, I say to you, unless one is born of water and the Spirit, he cannot enter the kingdom of God. That which is born of the flesh is flesh, and that which is born of the Spirit is spirit. Do*

not marvel that I say to you, 'You must be born again' "
(John 3:3–7).

To Nicodemus Jesus is saying that your natural birth
does not qualify you for the Kingdom of God. There needs to
be another experience, another birth, that is from above, a
heavenly birth. This spiritual birth is equivalent to the
Baptism of the Spirit. This birth comes about when we are
renewed in Jesus Christ. It is the Spirit that brings us into
relationship with Christ and He baptizes us and gives us a
new beginning with Christ. "The baptism of the Spirit is the
gift of life by which a man is admitted into the Kingdom of
God" (*Understanding the Holy Spirit*, 115).

When does the Baptism of the Holy Spirit Occur?

The best timeline for the Baptism of the Holy Spirit can be
seen at the baptism of Jesus. *And when Jesus was baptized, he
went up immediately from the water, and behold, the heavens
were opened and he saw the Spirit of God descending like a dove
and alighting on him* (Matthew 3:16). Christ is our perfect
example and as the gospel mentioned, the Spirit came upon
Him as soon as He was baptized. Baptism signifies the beginning of a new life. There must be a conversion before one is
baptized, and for the baptized person to maintain a relationship with God, one has to be controlled by the Spirit of God.
This controlling cannot take place before there is a total
surrender to Christ. "Self must be buried with Christ and we
must be baptized with the Holy Spirit of God. Then will be
revealed in speech, in spirit, and in our manner of labor the
fact that the Spirit of God is guiding" (*Evangelism*, 472).

As Christ spoke to Nicodemus, He said, *Unless one is
born of water and the Spirit, he cannot enter the Kingdom of
God* (John 3:5). Again, the Baptism of the Holy Spirit and the
baptism of water are closely associated. True conversion not
only leads to water baptism, but spiritual baptism. Both
experiences should go together.

Unfortunately there are some who receive the water
baptism and do not receive the Spirit's baptism. This was the

case in Ephesus when Paul arrived and found some disciples who were believers. *Paul said to them, "Did you receive the Holy Spirit when you believed?" And they said, "No, we have never even heard that there is a Holy Spirit." And he said, "Into what then were you baptized?" They said, "Into John's baptism." And Paul said, "John baptized with the baptism of repentance, telling the people to believe in the One who was to come after him, this is Jesus." On hearing this, they were baptized in the name of Jesus. And when Paul had laid his hands upon them, the Holy Spirit came on them, and they spoke with tongues and prophesied* (Acts 19:2–6).

From the question that Paul asked, one realizes that it was expected that these disciples were to have received the Holy Spirit when they first believed. However, their teacher, Apollos, a native of Alexandria who came to Ephesus and taught the teaching of John the Baptist, never understood the doctrine of the Holy Spirit. He was preaching in the synagogue...*but when Priscilla and Aquila heard him, they took him and expounded to him the way of God more accurately* (Acts 18;26).

These disciples evidently did not receive the full teaching of the gospel. Yet they were baptized according to John's baptism which was *the baptism of repentance, telling the people to believe in the one who was to come after him, that is, Jesus* (Acts 19:4). When Paul exposed them to the full gospel of Christ and the workings of the Holy Spirit, they were again baptized and subsequently received the Holy Spirit.

One of the chief lessons to be learned from the above experience is that when we learn of the gospel of Christ and accept its teachings and are baptized, we must also receive the Holy Spirit. It is the Spirit that will give one new life. It is the Spirit that will give one power to overcome temptations. It is the Spirit that will keep us until the appearing of our Lord and Saviour, Jesus Christ.

This baptism of the Holy Spirit must not be only a once-in-a-life-time experience. It must be a daily experience. Ellen White said, "From hours spent with God He came forth morning by morning, to bring the light of heaven to men.

Daily He received a fresh baptism of the Holy Spirit. In the early hours of the new day, the Lord awakened Him from His slumber and His soul and His lips were anointed with grace, that He might impart to others. His words were given Him fresh from the heavenly courts, words that He might speak in season to the weary and oppressed" (*Christ Object Lessons*, p. 132).

Why is the Baptism of the Holy Spirit Essential?

Without the baptism of the Spirit we cannot enter the kingdom of God. *Truly, truly I say to you, unless one is born of water and the Spirit, he cannot enter the kingdom of God. That which is born of the flesh is flesh, and that which is born of the Spirit is spirit* (John 3:5,6).

David said, *Behold, I was brought forth in iniquity and in sin did my mother conceive me* (Psalm 51:5).

Paul said, *All have sinned and fall short of the glory of God* (Romans 3:23). He further said, *For the wages of sin is death, but the free gift of God is eternal life in Christ Jesus our Lord* (Romans 6:23).

There is no hope for mankind if there is no change. In our natural condition we are destined to perish. There needs to be a rebirth, a renewal that is only experienced through Jesus Christ who has given us His Holy Spirit. We must be baptized into Christ through the Holy Spirit if we are to enter into His kingdom and enjoy eternal life.

It is the baptism of the Holy Spirit that restores the image of God in mankind. When Adam sinned he began to lose the image of God with which he was created (Genesis 1:26). Sin began to erode the imagery of God from man. The coming of Jesus was to bring about a restoration of God's image in us. This restoration is accomplished through the Holy Spirit. The Spirit's baptism begins a new work in the believer, a work that will continue until the coming of Jesus Christ.

How will the baptism of the Spirit affect the believer? As it was on the day of Pentecost, the baptism of the Spirit will

67

bring new life to the believer. "The baptism of the Holy Ghost, as on the day of Pentecost, will lead to a revival of true religion and to the performance of many wonderful works. Heavenly intelligence will come among us, and men will speak as they are moved upon by the Holy Spirit of God" (*Selected Messages*, Vol. 2, 57).

The apostles, after Pentecost, were filled with divine energy to do the will of God. They were everywhere proclaiming the message of a risen Christ. Nothing could deter them, even though they were persecuted, imprisoned and even killed. They did not refrain from telling the story of Jesus. "The hearts of the disciples were surcharged with a benevolence so full, so deep, so far-reaching, that it impelled them to go to the ends of the earth testifying: God forbid that we should glory, save in the cross of our Lord Jesus Christ. They were filled with an intense longing to add to the church such as should be saved. They called on the believers to arouse and do their part, that all nations might hear the truth and the earth be filled with the glory of the Lord." (*Testimonies to the Church*, Vol 7, 31, 32).

The baptism of the Holy Spirit will bring life and energy to the church. Many of our churches are dull and cold. Those who attend these churches enter and leave empty, nothing to sustain them throughout the week. This cold environment forms a fertile ground for the Devil to rob the believer of his/her experience with God. Too often we see individuals withered and dry from spiritual deficiency that result in a malnourished lifestyle. This is not God's plan for us.

"The atmosphere of the church is so frigid, its spirit is of such an order that men and women cannot sustain or endure the example of primitive and heaven-born piety. The warmth of their first love is frozen up, and unless they are watered over by the Baptism of the Holy Spirit, their candlestick will be removed out of its place, except they repent and do their first works" (*Testimonies to Ministers*, 167,168).

There needs to be a renewal of true godliness among the people of God. This cannot be realized unless the Holy Spirit is allowed to take full control of our lives. This the Spirit is waiting to do, but we need to empty our hearts of the selfish pride that clogs the avenues of our souls. The sooner we come to God in confession and repent of our sins, the quicker the Holy Spirit will bathe our souls with His peace. The baptism of the Spirit is God's gift, ready to be bestowed on all those whose hearts are prepared to receive it.

There is no need to tarry for the Baptism of the Holy Spirit. The Spirit of God is already in the world. What we need to do is to make room in our hearts to receive Him. He wants to enter our hearts to prepare us for the coming King. *If you then, who are evil, know how to give good gifts to your children, how much more will your Father who is in heaven give good things to those who ask him* (Matthew 7:11). God wants to bestow upon His children the most precious gift, the gift of the Holy Spirit. He gave Him to His disciples at Pentecost, and He is ready to give Him to everyone who will receive Him. The baptism of the Spirit will make ready the believers for the coming of the Lord.

Chapter Eleven

The Baptism with Fire

In the previous chapter we dealt with the baptism of the Holy Spirit. John not only spoke of the baptism with the Holy Spirit, but the baptism with fire. *I baptize you with water for repentance, but he who is coming after me is mightier than I, whose sandals I am not worthy to carry; He will baptize you with the Holy Spirit and with fire* (Matthew 3:11).

This prophecy of John concerning Jesus met its fulfillment at Pentecost. *And there appeared to them tongues as of fire, distributed and resting on each one of them. And they were all filled with the Holy Spirit and began to speak in other tongues, as the Spirit gave them utterance* (Acts 2:3,4).

The baptism with the Holy Spirit would appear easier to be understood than the baptism with fire. Is this the baptism that some require of those who desire membership in their fellowship, the baptism in which the person has to pass through literal fire to be accepted as a member? Or is this the fiery trial that we must endure throughout the Christian life? Is baptism with fire an alternative to the baptism of the Holy Spirit, or is this a complimentary experience at baptism?

Notice that the text in Matthew 3:11 says that *He will baptize you with the Holy Spirit AND with fire* (emphasis added), not baptize you with the Holy Spirit OR with fire. Froom said, "It is an explanatory phrase, complementing the idea. It is the Scriptural way of repetition to emphasize and enforce a single thought," (*Coming of the Comforter*, 268).

Ellen White, commenting on this text said, "The prophet Isaiah had declared that the Lord would cleanse His people from their iniquities 'by the spirit of judgment, and by the spirit of burning.' The word of the Lord to Israel was, 'I will turn My hand upon thee, and purely purge away thy dross, and take away all thy sin' (Isaiah 4:4; 1:25). To sin, wherever found, 'our God is a consuming fire' (Hebrews 12:29). In all who submit to His power the Spirit of God will consume sin. But if men cling to sin, they become identified with it. Then the glory of God, which destroys sin, must destroy them. Jacob, after his night of wrestling with the Angel, exclaimed, 'I have seen God face to face, and my life is preserved' (Genesis 32: 30). Jacob had been guilty of a great sin in his conduct toward Esau, but he had repented. His transgression had been forgiven, and his sin purged, therefore he could endure the revelation of God's presence. But wherever men came before God while willfully cherishing evil, they were destroyed. At the second advent of Christ the wicked shall be consumed 'with the Spirit of His mouth,' and destroyed 'with the brightness of His coming' (2 Thess. 2:8). The light of the glory of God, which imparts life to the righteous, will slay the wicked" (*Desire of Ages*, 107, 108).

Let us look for a moment on some of the ways that God used fire to relate to His people. At Eden's gate, God posted an angel with a flaming sword (Genesis 3:24). Moses saw the burning bush at Horeb when he heard the voice of God speaking to him (Exodus 3:2–4). Moses also received the law from God as fire enshrouded Sinai (Exodus 19:18). As the Children of Israel journeyed through the wilderness, God was represented by a pillar of fire that guided them through the night and warmed their chilly bodies (Exodus 13:21). To Elijah's prayer, He responded by sending fire from heaven and consuming the offering along with the stones that made up the altar and the water that was poured on the offering (I King 18:38). When the day of Pentecost came, the Holy Spirit came upon the disciples as tongues of fire and sat upon each of them (Acts 2:3).

Fire has played an important role in the way God taught His people. In the book of Isaiah, the prophet recorded: *When the Lord shall have washed away the filth of the daughters of Zion and cleansed the bloodstains of Jerusalem from its midst by a spirit of judgment and by a spirit of burning* (Isaiah

4:4). The writer of the book of Hebrews also said: *For our God is a consuming fire* (Hebrews 12:29).

Fire has been used in history as a dominant element. It is the most valuable physical force that we are aware of. Fire rightly represents God because God is the most dominant force in the world. More specifically, fire represents the Holy Spirit because He penetrates and purifies all who allow Him to enter their lives.

Fire as Used in the Sanctuary Ritual

Moses was instructed by God to *Let them build me a sanctuary that I may dwell in their midst* (Exodus 25:8). God clearly instructed Moses on how the sanctuary should be built, what the measurements should be, the colors, and the type of furniture that should be within it. God also instructed Moses concerning the offerings that should be offered in the sanctuary services and how these offerings should be performed.

Repeatedly we notice that these offerings were offered with fire (See Exodus 29:38–30:10). The paschal lamb was roasted in fire before it was eaten by the people. This lamb was symbolic of Christ, the Lamb of God who was offered on Calvary's tree. As we partake of the bread of the communion service, we must remember that the bread represents the body of Christ that was offered as a sacrifice for us who are sinners.

The sin offering was carried outside the camp and burned with fire as a symbol of our sins laid on Jesus Christ who was also crucified outside the gates of Jerusalem. It is the Spirit that awakens in us an awareness of our sins and leads us to Christ who alone can forgive us of our transgressions.

The burnt offering was consumed on the altar by fire as a symbol of our lives being laid on the altar of sacrifice. As we yield ourselves to God by the Holy Spirit, our lives will be accepted before Him as being truly consecrated—body, soul and spirit.

The peace offering was also offered with fire. In this offering the fat and the inner parts were given to God and consumed on the altar by fire. The shoulder and breast were given to the priest and eaten by him. These acts of giving to God and the priest were symbolic of the communion the sinner has with God through the Holy Spirit.

The grain offering was also an offering by fire. Fine flour mingled with oil and frankincense was baked in fire. It was also a type of Christ, our spiritual substance, nourishing and feeding us with His own life by the fire of the Holy Spirit.

The incense presented in the holy place was an offering with fire. The sweet spices were ground very small and mixed. This was burned in the golden censer and the sweet incense went up in a cloud of incense before the Lord. The fragrance filled the entire holy place with sweet perfume.

This offering represents the prayers of God's people, broken up in identical pieces, but each piece represents the different concerns of the people of God. The fire which consumed the incense represents the Holy Spirit who must take our prayers and form them in heavenly language and transmit them to the throne room of God. *The Holy Spirit helps us in our weakness; for we do not know how to pray as we ought, but the Spirit himself intercedes for us with sighs too deep for words. And he who searches the hearts of men knows what is the mind of the Spirit, because the Spirit intercedes for the saints according to the will of God* (Romans 8:26,27).

Lessons to Learn from Fire

1. Fire cleanses...

Fire is one of the most effective cleansing elements. "It differs from water in this, that, while water cleanses externally, fire purifies internally and intrinsically, penetrating to the very substance of things and filling every fiber and particle of matter with its own element" (*The Holy Spirit*, 86,87).

The baptism with water represents the cleaning of our lives and conduct, but the baptism of Christ by fire went deeper to the source of our conduct. It went to the very heart of the matter, the very source of our actions. Ezekiel the prophet said, *A new heart I will give you, and a new spirit I will put within you; and I will take out of your flesh the heart of stone and give you a heart of flesh* (36:26). Our actions spring from the heart (mind) and the heart must experience a change if the actions are going to change. The fire baptism then penetrates deeper than the surface to the very root of the issue.

I cannot forget growing up with my grandmother who did some farming to assist the economy of the home. In the early part of the year I would join the adults who were invited to clear the land for planting corn and peas. After they cut down the high bushes and some trees, they would pile the rubbish together in several heaps and light a fire to them. Before long there would be several fires that not only burned the various heaps, but the rest of the ground where we were to plant the corn and peas.

I never realized the importance of this process until much later. The fire was a cleansing agent for the ground where we were about to plant the seeds. The fire drove away all the rodents and killed the insects that could not or would not escape. This burning of the earth gave time for the seeds to germinate and grow to a reasonable height before insects would return and infest the area, thus making it easier for the plants to grow.

So is the working of the Holy Spirit in the life of the believer. The baptism with fire does a deep cleansing of the sinner's heart, destroying the rubbish that encumbers our minds, purifying our souls and providing a clean heart where growth can take place. Malachi pointed out that *He is like a refiner's fire and like fullers' soap* (3:2). God desires that the hearts of His children be clean. Through the Holy Spirit, like a flame He consumes the dross and leaves the heart pure. The Spirit separates us from the sinful life that perniciously dominates us, and implants into us a new nature, the nature of Christ.

We are told in Numbers 31:23 *Everything that can stand the fire, you shall pass through the fire.* The way to be made really clean is through the penetrating, purifying consuming fire of the Holy Spirit. We as believers need that cleansing fire to pass over and through us. This fire will penetrate every fiber of our being, and every secret chamber of our souls.

Before Pentecost the disciples were filled with selfishness. They were striving for supremacy, arguing for position, seeking to exalt self. But after Pentecost, what a difference came over the disciples! Now self was abased and a spirit of unity characterized each of them. Christ alone was first in their lives, and their desire now was only to lift up Jesus their Lord and Master.

This is the experience we must have today. As we embark on the last days of earth's history, self must also die and Christ must be exalted on the throne of our hearts. This the Spirit can accomplish in us, but He needs our consent to operate within us to cleanse us from all our sins.

2. Fire Reveals...

Now if any one builds on the foundation with gold, silver, precious stones, wood, hay, straw—each man's work will become manifest; for the day will disclose it, because it will be revealed with fire, and the fire will test what sort of work each one has done. If the work which any man has built on the foundation survives, he will receive a reward. If any man's work is burned up, he will suffer loss, though he himself will be saved, but only as through fire (I Corinthians 3:12–15).

The baptism with fire reveals a person as the individual really is. The baptism of fire will determine what we are really made of, whether wood, hay, straw, silver or gold. God desires that we be pure gold. Pure gold does not come about without a test. In fact, pure gold must be tested in a refiner's fire, a furnace hot enough to remove the dross and all useless material. It is only when the gold goes through the ultimate test that it can be said, "It is pure."

The child of God must go through the test of life, tried in the fiery trials that should drive us closer to God. The beauty is that as we go through these trials we do not have to go through them alone. Christ said *I am with you always, to the close of the age* (Matthew 28:20).

Christ Himself went through fiery trials in the wilderness with Satan, throughout His entire life on earth, even to His last days in the Garden of Gethsemane, and finally at His death on the cross. Yet He did not flinch. He did not lose hope. He depended on His heavenly Father and through the Holy Spirit He gained ultimate victory. This victory is for all those who put their trust in the Lord and depend on Him for overcoming power.

"When Jesus baptizes a man with the Holy Spirit and with fire, there is revealed an amount of pride, selfishness, suspiciousness, love of position, touchiness, and downright meanness that will be an amazement to him. When God baptizes my soul with fire, I come more and more to abhor myself. I sense increasingly that in me there is no good thing. All I have or am that is worth anything has been imputed and imparted to me from my Lord and Saviour Jesus Christ. It brings me to my knees before God in contrite confession" (*Coming of the Comforter*, 270).

3. Fire Breaks the Cord of Sin...

As we think about fire breaking the cords of sin, we recall the life of Samson as he drifted farther and farther from God. Samson was selected by God to be a judge of Israel and to deliver Israel from the hands of the Philistines. Samson, who received his strength from God, was determined to do things his own way. Before he knew it, Samson's life was bound up with the cords of sin. Delilah, who sought the secret of his strength, persuaded Samson until he was finally cornered by the Philistines. In one of the tricks he played with Delilah, Samson told her *If they bind me with seven fresh bowstrings which have not been dried, then I shall become weak, and be like any other man. Then the lords of the Philistines brought her seven fresh bowstrings which had not been dried, and she bound him with them. ...But he snapped the bowstrings, as a string of tow snaps when it touches the fire* (Judges 16:7–9).

Sin is binding men and women tighter than the bowstrings that bound Samson. Sin that cannot be snapped with our own strength. Satan is busy seeking out where we are weakest, and wherever he finds a weak point he tries to capitalize on it. He is seeking to tie our souls so tight that our energies will be sapped and our lives will be suffocated. But God will not stand by idle and let Satan have his way with us.

The sinner that cries out to God for help will have the immediate assistance of Divine power, the fire of the Holy Spirit to break the cords of the devil and set the captives free—free from fear and guilt, free from the bondage in which Satan delights to keep us. Christ came to set the captives free. He said, *The Spirit of the Lord is upon me, because he has anointed me to preach good news to the poor. He has sent me to proclaim release to the captives and recovering of sight to the blind, to set at liberty those who are oppressed, to proclaim the acceptable year of the Lord* (Luke 4:18,19).

God will not leave us entrapped by the devil. He will not forsake us, being entangled in his web. The Spirit of God is ready to loose us and let us go if we only reach out in faith and ask Him for help.

4. Fire Softens and Melts...

Fire goes before Him, and burns up his adversaries round about. His lightening lighten the world; the earth sees and trembles. The mountains melt like wax before the Lord, before the Lord of all the earth (Psalm 97:3–5). The fire of God's Holy Spirit is always before us, going in front doing the clearing and smoothing the path. The fire of the Holy Spirit takes on whatever the obstacle may be, even the mountains melt like wax. We are beset with mountains in our lives, mountains that separate us from God and create a gulf between us and our Maker. The Holy Spirit is able to melt those mountains down—those mountains of self, hardened wills and stony hearts. The Spirit of God is ready to break these barriers down.

There are mountains of prejudice and racial bigotry that divide us. We must let the Holy Spirit melt down these mountains so that we will have hearts of flesh, softened by His power, which will allow us to be fused together with our brethren in unity. Wherever there is a melting down, there results a oneness. As the lava of a volcano mingles together, so the lives of those who are baptized by the Spirit will be mingled together in love that is divine.

At Pentecost the disciples were in "one accord." This was the result of days of prayer, confession, repentance and forgiveness. The mountains that divided them were melted down with the power of the Holy Ghost. There was a oneness that they had never seen before, and what great work was accomplished as a result! We must repeat Pentecost daily in our lives. Why? Because the same Spirit that brought the disciples together is able to bring us together now so that there will be a harmony and a joy all around us and the cause of God will be advanced.

5. Fire Makes Permanent...

I counsel you to buy from me gold refined by fire, that you may be rich (Revelation 3:18). The process of preserving gold requires a melting and hardening. I can recall going to a very small gold mine in Zimbabwe, Africa. There the workers, before they would store away the gold, would wash the ore, separate the obvious strange particles, then heat the gold in fire, which melts it to a liquid. After that, this precious liquid was poured into containers where it would set in permanent form.

In the life of the believer, the fire of the Spirit will not only purify us, but will give us a permanence that can endure fiery trials. Fiery trails help to fit us for the task ahead. So, while the fire of the Holy Spirit removes the dross from our lives, it also makes us stronger to face the challenges of life.

The firing process of the Holy Spirit helps us to become permanent and impervious to the attacks of the wicked one. Paul asked the question, *Who shall separate us from the love of Christ? Shall tribulation, or distress, or persecution, or famine, or nakedness, or peril, or sword? As it is written, "For thy sake we are being killed all the day long; we are regarded as sheep to be slaughtered." No, in all these things we are more than conquerors through him who loved us. For I am sure that neither death, nor life, nor angels, nor principalities, nor things present, nor things to come, nor power, nor height, nor depth, nor anything else in all creation, will be able to separate us from the love of God in Christ Jesus our Lord* (Romans 8:35–39). Paul had been through many trials and temptations. He had been tested on every side, but he knew that he was resting in the love of Jesus Christ. Even though he had failed God in some areas of his life, God had never failed him. God's love was always constant; it was a permanent fixture that no creature or power could change.

We too can find that permanence in God. God's love never changes, it never falls short, it is sufficient. We might be battered by the Devil every day; he may accuse us of every sin, but we can find solace in the love of Christ. The Holy Spirit will establish us in the faith of Christ so that we can withstand the Devil.

The burning fire of the Holy Spirit must make a permanent impression on our heart. We need to be marked off and separated for His purpose. God desires to burn His seal upon our hearts as the herdsman burned his seal with his imprint upon his cattle. The seal of God's love must be evident as a claim on us for eternity. This seal of the Holy Spirit will give us permanence as the possession of God.

6. Fire is an Energizing Force...

Fire gives power. Fire is the source of power for many industries. The combustion chambers of engines are driven by fire. Fire is indispensable in our society.

The disciples on the day of Pentecost were ignited with the fire of the Holy Spirit. *And there appeared to them tongues of fire, distributed and resting on each one of them* (Acts 2:3). The Holy Spirit came upon the disciples as tongues of fire. The disciple needed the fire of God's Spirit to kindle the zeal they lacked. When Christ died, their hopes were doomed. They thought that the time of their mission to advance the Kingdom of God had passed. They were now returning to their previous trades. Instead of being fishers of men, some returned to be fishers of fish. Their zeal was stopped.

God, knowing the task He had assigned them, knew that they needed more than the warmth of a coal fire. They needed the Holy Ghost's fire to move them into action. There were thousands to be saved, and they needed changed hearts and a new spirit. The Holy Spirit came upon them as tongues of fire symbolizing that they needed to speak the word of Jesus with power, and as they went forth to speak, God would be there through the Holy Spirit to tell them what to say.

It was amazing how Peter presented such a powerful sermon that melted the hearts of sinners so much that they cried out, *Brethren, what shall we do?* (Acts 2:37). Peter responded, *Repent, and be baptized every one of you in the name of Jesus Christ, for the forgiveness of your sins; and you shall receive the gift of the Holy Ghost* (Acts 2:38). We are told that three thousand were baptized that day. Tremendous energy was released on the day of Pentecost. So much so that those who were assembled for the feast of Pentecost could not help but listen to the disciples as they proclaimed the name of Jesus as the Saviour of the world.

"The hearts of the disciples were surcharged with a benevolence so full, so deep, so far-reaching, that it impelled them to go to the ends of the earth testifying: God forbid that we should glory, save in the cross of our Lord Jesus Christ. They were filled with an intense longing to add to the church, such as should be saved. They called on the believers to arouse and do their part, that all nations might hear the truth and the earth be filled with the glory of the Lord.

By the grace of Christ, the apostles were made what they were. It was sincere devotion and humble earnest prayer that brought them into close communion with Him. They sat together with Him in heavenly places. They realized the greatness of their debt to Him. By earnest, persevering prayer they obtained the endowment of the Holy Spirit, and then they went forth, weighted with the burden of saving souls, filled with zeal to extend the triumphs of the cross. And under their labors, many souls were brought from darkness to light, and many churches were raised up" (*Testimonies to the Church*, Vol. 7, 31,32).

"After the descent of the Holy Spirit, the disciples were so filled with love for Him and for those for whom He died, that hearts were melted by the words they spoke and the prayers they offered. They spoke in the power of the Spirit;

and under the influence of that power, thousands were converted" (*Acts of the Apostles*, 22).

Today we need this energizing force to awaken us from our lethargy. Thousands, yea millions, are dying and entering Christless graves. Too long the church has been laden down with things that are not eternal, and many are deterred from their real purpose. The real purpose of the church is to proclaim the gospel of a crucified, risen, and returning Lord. This is our only mission, and we need the baptism of the Holy Spirit's fire to accomplish this task.

The Holy Spirit can ignite our frozen bones and warm our cold hearts to get us on the move for God and shed light on the path of those who are still in darkness. The prophet Jeremiah said, *There is in my heart as it were a burning fire shut up in my bones, and I am weary with holding it in, and I cannot* (Jeremiah 20:9).

How can we taste of the Water of Life and not invite others to drink? How can we eat of the Bread of Life and not ask our neighbors to come and eat also? How can we conceal the word of God in our hearts while others are dying for some words of life? Let the energy of the Holy Spirit flow through us and energize those we come in contact with. God is counting on us!

Chapter Twelve

The Former and Latter Rains

The Former Rain

And it shall come to pass afterward, that I will pour out my Spirit on all flesh; your sons and your daughters shall prophesy, your old men will dream dreams, your young men shall see visions. Even upon the menservants and maidservants in those days, I will pour out my Spirit (Joel 2:28,29). What took place at Pentecost was a partial fulfillment of this prophecy by the prophet Joel. "This prophecy received a partial fulfillment in the outpouring of the Spirit on the day of Pentecost; but it will reach its full accomplishment in the manifestation of divine grace which will attend the closing work of the gospel" (*The Great Controversy*, 11).

Pentecost began a new era in the Christian church. It was on the day of Pentecost that the Holy Spirit came upon the small band of disciples, a hundred and twenty in number, and supplied them with a power they had never felt before. "Christ's ascension to heaven was the signal that His followers were to receive the promised blessing. For this they were to wait before they entered upon their work. When Christ passed within the heavenly gates, He was enthroned amidst the adoration of angels. As soon as this ceremony was completed, the Holy Spirit descended upon the disciples in rich currents, and Christ was indeed glorified, even with the glory which He had with the Father from all eternity. The Pentecostal outpouring was Heaven's communication that the Redeemer's inauguration was accomplished. According to His promise He had sent the Holy Spirit from heaven to His followers as a token that He had, as priest and king, received all authority in heaven and on earth, and was the Anointed One over His people" (*Acts of the Apostles*, 38,39).

The early church received this promised blessing which gave it its divine commencement in the new era. This spiritual explosion could not have come at a better time. The Jews attending the Feast of Pentecost in Jerusalem came from various parts of the Mediterranean world. These Jews who spoke the languages of the territories where they lived, came to Jerusalem to offer their personal sacrifices. But they were amazed at what they saw. They heard the followers of Jesus speaking in their own native languages (Acts 2:4). The message of Jesus Christ was proclaimed clearly and all those who listened heard the gospel for themselves. The gospel seed did not only stay in Jerusalem, but through these Jews and now multilingual disciples, the gospel was carried to the then-known world.

In the eastern countries, the former rain falls at sowing time. This rain is necessary that the seed may germinate. As a result, these early showers cause the tender shoots to spring up and progressively grow to maturity. The latter rain comes near the close of the season when the plants are mature and close to ripening. This final shower prepares the grains for the harvest. God uses the cycle of nature frequently to illustrate how He works with His people. As the rain is given first to help the seed germinate and then later to prepare it for harvest, so the Lord sends His Spirit to first germinate within our souls, and then to cause us to grow from one stage to another. Christ seeks to complete His work within us as individuals and the Church in general. He will send the latter rain within our hearts to prepare us for His final harvest.

"Unless the former rain has fallen, there will be no life and the green blade will not spring up. Unless the early showers have done their work, the latter rain can bring no seed to perfection" (*Testimonies to Ministers*, 506).

"Many have in great measure failed to receive the former rain. They have not obtained all the benefits that God has thus provided for them. They expect that the lack will be supplied by the latter rain. When the richest abundance of grace shall be bestowed, they intend to open their hearts to receive it. They are making a terrible mistake. It is God who began the work, and He will finish His work, making men complete in Jesus Christ. But there must be no neglect of the grace represented by the former rain. Only those who are living up to the light they have will receive greater light. Unless we are daily advancing in the exemplification of active Christian witness, we shall not recognize the manifestation of the Holy Spirit in the latter rain. It may be falling on hearts around us, but we shall not discern or receive it" (*Testimonies to Ministers*, 507).

Every Christian must receive the early or former rain of God's Spirit. It is this experience that we will be able to look back upon when the tempter throws us down into discouragement. We may call this former rain our "first love," the love we had when we first met the Lord. It is the Holy Spirit that softens our hearts, that we may be able to receive the riches of His blessings. We must all have our own Pentecost, a time when we seek after God with a contrite heart, when we come to God seeking forgiveness of sin and falling on the Rock, Christ Jesus. Through His Spirit, we are reshaped and healing to our souls is brought. The Christian life is a process. It begins only as a seed, but when that seed is watered and germinated by the Spirit, it will spring forth in abundance if we constantly depend on the Lord of harvest.

"Are we striving with all our power to attain to the stature of men and women in Christ? Are we seeking for His fullness, ever pressing toward the mark set before us—the perfection of His character? When the Lord's people reach this mark, they will be sealed in their foreheads. Filled with the Spirit, they will be complete in Christ, and the recording angel will declare, 'It is finished' " (Ellen G. White Comments, *SDA Bible Commentary*, Vol. 6, 1118).

It is the Holy Spirit that begins spiritual growth within our hearts. He follows the process every step of the way and He will bring our lives to the fullness which is only in Christ and make us ready for the second advent of our Lord and Saviour Jesus Christ.

The Latter Rain

Ask rain from the Lord in the season of the spring rain, from the Lord who makes the storm clouds, who gives men showers of rain, to everyone the vegetation in the field (Zechariah 10:1). The time of the latter rain is upon us. It is this rain that is to prepare the field for the harvest of the Lord. Pentecost was a partial fulfillment of the prophecy of Joel, *And it shall come to pass afterward that I will pour out my Spirit upon all flesh* (Joel 2:28). The disciples received the divine unction to carry out the mission that was assigned them, and they did it. We also need the divine unction to give the message of Christ its final sound. "The outpouring of the Spirit in the apostolic days was the 'former rain' and glorious was the result. But the latter rain will be more abundant" (*Manuscript Release*, Vol. 2, 44). We are living in the time of the end and this prophecy of Joel will find its fulfillment in these last days.

"Near the close of earth's harvest, a special bestowal of spiritual grace is promised to prepare the church for the coming of the Son of Man. This outpouring of the Spirit is likened to the falling of the latter rain; and it is for this added power that Christians are to send their petitions to the Lord of the harvest 'in the time of the latter rain.' In response 'the Lord shall make bright clouds, and give them showers of rain.' 'He will cause to come down ... the rain, the former rain, and the latter rain.' But unless the members of God's church today have a living connection with the Source of all spiritual growth, they will not be ready for the time of reaping. Unless they keep their lamps trimmed and burning, they will fail of receiving added grace in times of special need" (*Acts of the Apostles*, 55).

The adversary of our souls is working at jet speed to secure the souls of men. The Devil is wroth with the people of God and is using all available forces to overcome them. *Rejoice then, O heaven and you that dwell therein! But woe to you, O earth and sea, for the devil has come down to you in great wrath, because he knows that his time is short!* (Revelation 12:12). As the Devil intensifies his attacks on the people of God, the Spirit is made available for the hour of greatest temptation. It is necessary that we avail ourselves of His power to overcome the Devil. Satan fears those who empty themselves of sin and allow Christ to reign within.

"There is nothing that Satan fears so much as that the people of God shall clear the way by removing every hindrance, so that the Lord can pour out His Spirit upon a languishing church and an impenitent congregation. If Satan had his way, there would never be another awakening, great or small, to the end of time. But we are not ignorant of his devices. It is possible to resist his power. When the way is prepared for the Spirit of God, the blessing will come. Satan can no more hinder a shower of blessing from descending upon God's people than he can close the windows of heaven that rain cannot come upon the earth. Wicked men and devils cannot hinder the work of God, or shut out His presence from the assemblies of His people, if they will, with subdued, contrite hearts, confess and put away their sins, and in faith claim His promises. Every temptation, every opposing influence, whether open or secret, may be successfully resisted, 'not by might, nor by power, but by my Spirit, saith the Lord of hosts" (*Selected Messages*, Vol 1, 124).

The latter rain must not only prepare us for the harvest but must empower us for the final proclamation of God's call to the world. Everyone who receives a call to come to Jesus also has a responsibility to, in turn, tell someone else of Jesus and His saving power. The latter rain is given for us to bear our testimonies to those who are still in darkness. When Isaiah was touched by the live coal from the altar he went forth to witness for God. *Then flew one of the seraphim to me, having in his hand a burning coal which he had taken with tongs from the altar. And he touched my mouth, and said: "Behold, this has touched your lips; your guilt is taken away, and your sin is forgiven." And I heard the voice of the Lord saying, "Whom shall I send, and who will go for us?" Then I said, "Here am I! Send me"* (Isaiah 6:6–8).

God is ready to send the latter rain upon individuals and upon the church, but He is waiting for us to be ready to receive it. In Manuscript 24, page 4, 1896, Ellen White said, "When the laborers have an abiding Christ in their own souls, when all selfishness is dead, when there is no rivalry, no strife for supremacy, when oneness exists, when they sanctify themselves, so that love for one another is seen and felt, then the showers of the grace of the Holy Spirit will just as surely come upon them as that God's promise will never fail one jot or tittle. But when the work of others is discounted, that the workers may show their own superiority, they prove that their own work does not bear the signature it should, and God cannot bless them."

In another manuscript, Ellen White said, "If all those that handle the Word of God, ministering to people, cleanse their hearts from all iniquity and all defilement, and shall come to God with clean purpose of heart, as little children, they shall see of the salvation of God. Jesus will walk in our midst. We have now the invitation of mercy to become vessels unto honor, and then we need not worry about the latter rain; all we have to do is to keep the vessel clean and prepared and right side up, for the reception of the heavenly rain and keep praying, 'Let the rain come into my vessel. Let the light of the glorious angel which unites with the third angel, shine upon me, give me a part in the work, let me sound the proclamation, let me be a co-laborer with Jesus Christ" (Manuscript 35, 1891, 16).

The work of God in this earth will soon be over. Heaven will soon burst open and the Sun of Righteousness will come with a "sharp sickle" in his hand to reap the harvest. The people of God must arise now to give the trumpet its last sound. Prophecies are fulfilling all around us. 'The night is far spent and the day is at hand.' We need to go forward now in the power of the Spirit and tell the good news of the coming King.

The final work will be similar to the day of Pentecost. "Servants of God, with their faces lighted up and shining with holy consecration, will hasten from place to place to proclaim the message from heaven. By thousands of voices, all over the earth, the warning will be given. Miracles will be wrought, the sick will be healed, and signs and wonders will follow the believers" (*The Great Controversy*, 612).

Do not lose out on this blessing. Christ has promised it to us and it is about to fall. May we be ready to receive it so that we are not left out when others receive it. There is an abundance in the storehouse of heaven. The Holy Spirit wants to enter our hearts and fill us with His abundant grace. May our hearts be open to receive Him so that we may have power to do His will and be ready for the soon-appearing of our Lord and Saviour Jesus Christ.

Chapter Thirteen

The Holy Spirit's Last Message

In the last book of the Bible and the last chapter, a most profound invitation is given. *The Spirit and the Bride say, 'come.' And let him who hears say, 'come.' And let him who is thirsty, come, let him who desires take of the water of life without price* (Revelation 22:17). This invitation is the final cry of both the Holy Spirit and the church, the bride of Christ, to the sinner to come to Christ. It is noteworthy that the Holy Spirit did not singularly extend the invitation, but He is active through the church, leading men and women to the Saviour.

This invitation is a universal call to all who would respond to the beckoning of the Holy Spirit. The Spirit is calling, He is calling through the church, He is calling through the repentant sinner and His call is given freely to all to come to the Saviour Jesus Christ.

In Revelation chapters two and three, the message to each of the seven churches concludes with *He who has an ear, let him hear what the Spirit says to the churches.* The seven churches represent the period of time between Christ's ascension and Christ's second coming. During this period of time, the church has been going through many changes. As the passages indicate, there have been good times and bad times, but the Holy Spirit never abandoned the church. He is always wooing the church to come to Christ.

The last two messages of our Master before His ascension are recorded in the first eleven verses of the book of Acts. The messages are the promises of the Holy Spirit and the second coming of Christ. The coming of the Holy Spirit is a prerequisite to the second coming of Christ. The Holy Spirit was given to prepare the bride for the coming of the Bridegroom. Ever since that time, the work of preparation has been going on and the invitation has been given at every stage of the church for sinners to repent and come to Christ.

The Spirit has been working for centuries through the Bible prophets, pointing to the second coming of Christ as the climax of the age. "It was He who whispered to Enoch the first testimony respecting the advent in antediluvian times. It was He who gave dying Jacob his vision of Shiloh's reign. It was He who revealed, even to double-hearted Balaam, the glory of the latter days, until he longed to have part in it. It was He who enabled Job to speak of the days when in his flesh he would behold his living Redeemer and see Him for himself and not for another. It was He who inspired the heart of David to sing so often and so sublimely of the Prince of Peace whose name should endure forever and whose sway should reach from shore to shore. It was He who gave to Isaiah his prophet fire, and revealed to Daniel and Zechariah the panorama of the ages. Through the lips of the Master on the side of Olivet, He pre-told the fall of Jerusalem and the end of the age" (*The Holy Spirit*, 590–591).

He Predicts the Second Coming

"It was He who taught the early church this blessed hope of the comfort of her sorrows and the inspiration of her labors. It was He who gave to the first Apostolic Council at Jerusalem its clear outlined plan for the Christian age, and revealed to Paul the great apostasy and the glorious message of the advent in the epistles of Corinthians and Thessalonians. And now to the last of the apostles, He has unfolded with a clearness far surpassing all former visions, the glorious truth of the Lord's return" (*The Holy Spirit*, 590,591).

As we read in the Bible, in the first book, Genesis, we recognize that sin thwarted the plans that God had for man. God did not give up on mankind. In fact, He gave us the great promise of the Messiah who would defeat the devil and

92

restore mankind. *I will put enmity between you and the woman, and between your seed and her seed; he shall bruise your head, and you shall bruise his heel* (Genesis 3:15).

This promise was fulfilled at Calvary's cross on which the Saviour hung and died. From the grave He was resurrected and promised that He is coming again. The Holy Spirit came in His fullness at Pentecost to prepare the world for Christ's return. He is working through every born-again child of God to echo this message to those who are in darkness.

How to Proclaim the Message of the Advent

Paul has set the example of how we are to approach the proclamation of the message of our Lord. He said, *For I am not ashamed of the gospel: it is the power of God for salvation to everyone who has faith, to the Jews first and also to the Greek* (Romans 1:16). The Apostle Paul was on a mission, a mission made clear to him by the Spirit of God. He never went to the right nor to the left. He kept his eyes on the Lord Jesus Christ and became the leading mouthpiece for the gospel in the New Testament period.

"The hearts of the disciples were surcharged with a benevolence so full, so deep, so far-reaching, that it impelled them to go to the ends of the earth testifying: 'God forbid that I should glory, save in the cross of our Lord Jesus Christ.' They were filled with an intense longing to add to the church of such as should be saved. They called on the believers to arise and do their part, that all nations might hear the truth and the earth be filled with the glory of the Lord" (*Testimonies to the Church*, Vol. 7, 31).

With hearts burning with the flame of the Holy Spirit the disciples went forth with the gospel. Nothing could stop them, neither whips nor the jailing of church leaders. Neither stones nor Sanhedrin could hinder them. They spoke with boldness and did many wonders before the people.

As the message of Christ is being proclaimed today, no less energy or enthusiasm should accompany our effort. The same power that was available to those disciples is available to us. Men and women are dying in sin; corruption is rampant and iniquity has gone beyond measurable proportions. We cannot slow down now. The vision must be recaptured and we must tap into the same divine power and go forward without delay and give the loud cry.

He Awakens Desires for Christ's Return

In the gospel of John the Saviour's words are recorded: *And when he comes, he will convince the world concerning sin and righteousness and judgment* (John 16:8). The Holy Spirit's work has no boundaries. It encompasses the whole earth. No one can limit His power or His presence. He is drawing the world to Christ in preparation for His return.

When Christ came to earth as a babe almost two thousand years ago, the leaders of the Jews were not prepared for His coming, neither did they prepare the people to receive Him. It was wise men from the East who studied prophecies and knew the exact season when He was to be born. They followed the star to the place where He was to be born and finding Christ, they worshipped Him (Matthew 2:9–11). These wise men were guided by the Holy Spirit as they studied the Scriptures to understand the prophecies pointing to His birth.

No other parable seems to more aptly describe the second coming of Jesus than the parable of the ten virgins. All ten were waiting for the appearance of the Bridegroom. Five of them had extra oil with their lamps and the other five had taken no extra oil. These latter virgins went to the other five to get some of their oil, but the five refused saying they needed it for themselves lest they should also be in want. The five foolish virgins went to buy oil and when they were gone, the Bridegroom came and those who had extra oil went with the Bridegroom. When the foolish virgins returned, it was too late. They could not go in to be with the Bridegroom (Matthew 25:1–13).

The Bridegroom (Christ) is soon to return, and it may seem that He is delaying. Some will fail to be ready when He comes, but there are many who have yielded to the working of the Holy Spirit who will be ready to welcome Him when he returns to earth again. As the Spirit prepared the wise men for the first coming of Jesus, so in the same manner, He is preparing those who are wise for the second coming of Jesus. Those who would accept His invitation and come to Christ will be ready to meet Him when He returns to receive His Church again.

The Invitation

This final call of the Spirit should be taken personally. The Holy Spirit is focusing on each of us to not only respond to His invitation for personal salvation, but also for us to in turn invite others to come. This appeal does not discriminate; all are invited to come to Him, whatever the nationality or ethic background. There is room at the cross for all.

When Christ was leaving His disciples, He told them, *Let not your hearts be troubled; believe in God, believe also in me. In my Father's house are many rooms; if it were not so, would I have told you that I go to prepare a place for you? And when I go and prepare a place for you, I will come again and will take you to myself that where I am you may be also* (John 14:1–3).

Christ is now preparing these "good rooms" for us in His kingdom, and His greatest desire is to see us coming to live in these prepared places. Not only is this a call to us to come and occupy these heavenly places, but to bring others with us.

Paul said, *I appeal to you therefore, brethren, by the mercies of God, to present your bodies as a living sacrifice, holy and acceptable to God, which is your spiritual worship* (Romans 12:1). As we face these last days and the final call of God for men and women to come out of darkness into His marvelous light, we must consecrate ourselves completely to God. God cannot effectively use us except we yield ourselves unreservedly to Him.

"It is not enough to give monies to churches in the form of tithes and offerings. It is time that we give ourselves in complete dedication. It is time for the experience of the disciples in the days of ancient Jerusalem to be renewed in the church of today. It is time that ministers, church officers, and church members unite forces and work together on bended knees for the outpouring of the showers of the latter rain" (Wesley Amundsen, *Power of Pentecost*, 100).

"He, Jesus, gave His Church one thing—only one—to do. That was to go into all the world and preach this gospel to every creature, teaching them everything He had taught His disciples. This is the one mission of the Church. It is the one great objective of all Christian endeavor. The Church has no business undertaking anything else. Every church house we build, every school, college or university we erect and endow, every sermon we preach, every prayer we offer, every lesson we teach, every social service act we render—all that Christians can do—should have as its ultimate objective the carrying out of the great commission Jesus gave to His followers—to go into all the world and preach the gospel to every creature" (Bishop O. E. Goddard, *The Methodist Evangel*, 101,102).

The challenge of sharing the good news of salvation is ours; the privilege is awesome and the process is rewarding. The Lord has even promised that we do not have to walk this journey alone. He will be there to guide us even to the end. What an awesome opportunity to be co-laborers with Christ through the power of the Holy Spirit, to proclaim the everlasting gospel of God.

"Servants of God, with their faces lighted up and shining with holy consecration, will hasten from place to place to proclaim the message from heaven. By thousands of voices, all over the earth, the warning will be given. Miracles will be wrought, the sick will be healed, and signs and wonders will follow the believers. Satan also works with lying wonders, even bringing down fire from heaven in the sight of men. Thus the inhabitants of the earth will be brought to take their stand" (*The Great Controversy*, 612).

There is a glorious hope still before us. That is the hope of the coming of the Lord in power and glory, coming for those who have made the choice to give their all to Him. Surely the devil is working diligently to draw as many as he can to himself, but the power of the Holy Spirit has more "magnetic force" in the drawing of men and women who would yield their souls to Christ. Christ cannot draw us to Himself if we are not surrendered to Him. He will not force us beyond our will, because the power of choice is a gift He has given to us, never to be retaken. Whenever we express a willingness to come to Him, the Spirit of God will draw us with the cords of His love. *And I, when I am lifted up from the earth, will draw all men to myself* (John 12:32).

As the Spirit and the bride are calling sinners to come to Christ, and those who respond to the invitation in return call others to Christ, let us pray the prayer of John the Revelator, *Come, Lord Jesus* (Revelation 22:20).

Chapter Fourteen

Experiencing the Holy Spirit's Power

The study of the Holy Spirit is one of the most important experiences that anyone can ever have. It is virtually impossible that this experience will not deeply impact one's life. You see, the Holy Spirit is not a force, He is a Person, the third member of the Godhead. He was there at creation, He was there throughout the patriarchal age. He was there with Christ from His incarnation to His death. In fact, Christ was placed in Mary's womb by the Holy Spirit. He was poured out on the Church at Pentecost and since that time, He has been preparing the Church for the return of Jesus Christ.

Tony Evans said, "The Holy Spirit is not merely a nice addendum to the Christian faith. He is at the heart of it. He is not merely a force or an influence, He is the third Person of the Trinity, God Himself. If there is anything you and I must understand, if we are going to live what is commonly called the victorious Christian life, it is through the Person and ministry of the Holy Spirit" (*The Promise*, 15).

For me, this study has not only informed me of the Person and workings of the Holy Spirit, but it has transformed my life and granted me a renewed baptism of the Holy Spirit's power. As we go through this last chapter I will seek to unfold my experience of the power of the Holy Spirit.

Experience His Power in Prayer

Ellen White rightly said, "By the grace of Christ the apostles were made what they were. It was sincere devotion and humble, earnest prayer that brought them into close communion with Him. They sat together with Him in heavenly places. They realized the greatness of their debt to Him. By correct, persevering prayer they obtained the endowment of the Holy Spirit, and then they went forth weighted with the burden of saving souls, filled with zeal to extend the triumphs of the cross. And under their labors many souls were brought from darkness to light, and many churches were raised up.

"Shall we be less earnest than were the apostles? Shall we not by living faith, claim the promises that moved them to the depths of their being to call upon the Lord Jesus for the fulfillment of His word: 'Ask, and ye shall receive'? (John 16:24). Is not the Spirit of God to come today in answer to earnest, persevering prayer, and fill men with power? Is not God saying today to His praying, trusting, believing workers who are opening the Scriptures to those ignorant of the precious truth they contain: 'Lo, I am with you always, even unto the end of the world' (Matthew 28:20). Why, then is the church so weak and spiritless?" (*Testimonies to the Church*, Vol. 7, 32).

As I meditate on these statements, I ask myself, Have I been fervent in persevering prayer? Have I been emptying myself of the things that separate me from God? Have I been as earnest and sincere as I should be? I must confess, it was not what it should be. I thank my God who in His mercies kept beckoning me to come up a little higher. I have greater joy in the Lord today than I have ever had.

A life of prayer is a pre-requisite to this experience. I have not yet attained to the point I believe God desires me to be, but praise be to God, I have learned to depend on Him more. Getting up early in the morning, spending time with God in prayer, gives added strength to meet the day's challenges. It is also essential to maintain an attitude of prayer all day, because the devil will look for the slightest opportunity to squeeze himself into our lives and plant the seed of unrighteousness.

If you are in an attitude of prayer all day, then when the day is over and you look back on how God has led you, there will spring from your life praises and adoration for what He has done. "Those who are often in prayer have holy angels by their sides. The atmosphere that surrounds their souls is pure and holy; for their whole world is imbued with the sanctifying influence of the Spirit of God" (*Fundamentals of Christian Education*, 430).

As I take more time with God each day, I have come to realize that before I speak I seek the guidance of the Holy Spirit more often. There is more certainty in what I say, and I do not feel alone as I face the enemy of souls each day. A constant communion with God brings the soul into union with Him and like Paul said, *It is no longer I who lives, but Christ who lives in me; and the life I now live in the flesh I live by faith in the Son of God, who loved me and gave himself for me* (Galatians 2:20).

One of the great examples of a praying servant is Jacob. As recorded in Genesis, Jacob had treated his brother Esau unfairly. He had robbed him of this birthright. Esau saw himself stripped of everything that would establish him as inheritor of his father's, Isaac's possessions. He directed his anger at Jacob and planned to kill him because Jacob had caused him much pain.

Jacob realized that his only hope was in the Lord. So being left alone in the night, he agonized with God. He cried out to the Lord, *Deliver me, I pray thee, from the hand of my brother, from the hand of Esau, for I fear him, lest he come and slay us all, the master with the children* (Genesis 32:11). God heard his prayer and visited with him that night, and the Bible says, *A man wrestled with him until the breaking of the day. When the man saw that he did not prevail against Jacob, he touched the hollow of his thigh; and Jacob's thigh was put out of joint as he wrestled with him. Then he said, "Let me go, for the day is breaking." But Jacob said, "I will not let you go, unless you bless me"* (Genesis 32:28).

The experience of Jacob can be ours today if we seek the Lord with all our hearts and all our souls. God will come down to us and bless us abundantly, far and above all that we can ask or think. I thank God that we can be one with Him in prayer and receive power to do His will.

Experience His Power in Daily Living

In this rat-race society in which people are trying to survive, they sometimes forget that their success does not solely depend on themselves. The children of God also face this situation in which we can become so self-dependent that we forget that our strength comes from God.

Living just outside of New York City, I have also come in contact with the hustle and bustle of city life. Things can move so fast, and there are so many demands that if I do not stop in the midst of it all and evaluate what is really happening, I can forget that it is essential to listen to the voice of God every moment as I go about my daily activities.

Leaving home without taking time in private devotion and family worship results in a feeling of emptiness and uncertainty as I face the day's challenges. How can we go through life day by day without drinking from the fountain of God's grace, and receive spiritual supplies to take us along? I now thank God that more than ever before I see the need for a daily refreshing of the Holy Spirit as I face life's journey. "Morning by morning, as the heralds of the gospel kneel before the Lord and renew their vows of consecration to Him, He will grant them the presence of His Spirit, with its reviving, sanctifying power. As they go forth to the day's duties, they have the assurance that the unseen agency of the Holy Spirit enables them to be laborers together with God" (*Acts of the Apostles*, 56).

In the process of learning to trust in God daily, I recount my first trip to Canada from my home country, Jamaica, in 1975. I had never before flown in an airplane and my greatest fear was that during the flight I would not be able to control my circumstances. It was quite a lesson for me to sit in that airplane knowing I had to be there for about four hours, totally dependent on the knowledge and experience of the pilot to fly the aircraft to its destination. Each time I look back on that experience, it reminds me that in life's journey I have to let go of self and totally depend on Christ, through the Holy Spirit, to guide me through life's circumstances. It is not always easy to let go of self. It is one of the most difficult undertakings. However, that is what is required if we are going to let God control our lives fully. For only then will we be able to resist the devil and gain victory over him. "It is only by personal union with Christ, by communion with Him daily, hourly, that we can bear the fruits of the Holy Spirit" (*Testimonies to the Church*, Vol. 5, 48).

Experience His Power in the Study of His Word

...*No prophecy ever came by the impulse of man, but men moved by the Holy Spirit spoke from God* (2 Peter 1:21). The Holy Spirit was the mover on the hearts of the Bible writers as they penned the Scriptures. He inspired them to record the profound truths which guide us today. This self same Spirit will be with us as we study His Word to make applications to our own experiences.

I have read the Scriptures many times, but never before have I read them so systematically and intentionally as I have done over the past twelve months. This has resulted in a peace and tranquillity that I have never experienced before. There is power in the study of God's Word! As we teach or preach the Word of God, angels attend us and the Spirit brings back to our minds the powerful truths we have studied. I have seen lives changed from despair to hope; from darkness to light, as a result of the knowledge of the Word of God.

"The words of the Master Worker should be diligently studied; for they are spirit and life. Laborers who are striving to work in harmony with this instruction are under the leadership and guidance of the Holy Spirit, and need always, before they make any advance move, first ask permission of Someone else. No precise lines are to be laid down. Let the Holy Spirit direct the workers. As they keep looking unto Jesus, the Author and Finisher of their faith, the gift of grace will increase by wise use" (*Testimonies to Ministers* 492).

A life of total dependence on the Holy Spirit and submission to His word results in a life of victory. David said, *Thy word is a lamp to my feet and a light to my path* (Psalm

119:105). The assurance that our lives are guided by the Word of God is a wonderful feeling!

Experience His Power in Preaching

As a preacher for about twenty year, I would be lying if I told you that many times as I stand before hundreds and thousands of people, my heart is not overcome with fear, a fear that weakens my body and ties my tongue. That fear is planted by the Devil himself as he seeks to make me ineffective in the proclamation of the Word of God. It is only as I allow self to die and Christ be made alive in me that the spirit of fear vanishes.

Prior to Pentecost the apostles were also fearful. In fact, John records *On the evening of that day, the first day of the week, the doors being shut where the disciples were, for fear of the Jews, Jesus came and stood among them and said to them, "Peace be with you"* (John 20:19).

After Pentecost these same apostles were changed. They preached the gospel with boldness everywhere they went. In the book of Acts it is recorded, *Now when they saw the boldness of Peter and John, and perceived that they were uneducated, common men, they wondered; and they recognized that they had been with Jesus* (Acts 4:13). Further on in the same chapter it is noted that *when they had prayed, the place in which they were gathered together was shaken; and they were all filled with the Holy Spirit and spoke the word of God with boldness* (verse 31).

The Spirit of God is able to ignite a fire in the soul of the ministering servant of God, that those who hear the word proclaimed will realize that it cannot be the human agent but the Spirit speaking through an earthly vessel. This will be the experience of those who feed upon the Word of God and are baptized by His Spirit.

The heart that receives the Word of God is not as a pool that evaporates, not like a broken cistern that loses its treasure. It is like the mountain stream fed by unfailing springs, whose cool, sparkling water, leaps from rock to rock, refreshing the weary, the thirsty, the heavy laden.

"This experience gives every teller of truth the very qualifications that will make him a representative of Christ. The Spirit of Christ's teaching will give a force and directness to His communications and to his prayer. His witness to Christ will not be a narrow, lifeless testimony. The minister will not preach over and over the same set discourse. His mind will be open to constant illumination of the Holy Spirit. Christ said, 'Whoso eateth My flesh and drinketh My blood, hath eternal life...As the living Father hath sent me, and I live by the Father; so he that eateth Me, even he shall live by Me .... It is the Spirit that quickeneth. The words that I speak unto you, they are spirit, and they are life' (John 6:54–57, 63, KJV).

"When we eat Christ's flesh and drink His blood, the element of eternal life will be found in the ministry. There will not be a fund of stale, oft-repeated ideas. The tame, dull sermonizing will cease. The old truths will be presented, but they will be seen in a new light. There will be a new perception of truth, a clearness and a power that all will discern. Those who have the privilege of sitting under such a minister will, if susceptible to the Holy Spirit's influence, feel the energizing power of a new life. The fire of God's love will be kindled within them. Their perceptive faculties will be quickened to discern the beauty and majesty of truth" (*Christ's Object Lessons*, 130–132).

There are times when preachers get bogged down with the smallest details in their preaching. Everything must be so streamlined that there is little room for anything, even what is fresh from the Spirit. While it is good and responsible to prepare sermons ahead of schedule, we must realize that the Holy Spirit is still at work, even when the sermon is being preached. The Spirit is available to give us added power far beyond what we anticipated.

Ellen White said, "Some of these ministers make a mistake in the preparation of their discourses. They arrange every minutia with such exactness that they give the Lord no room to lead and impress their minds. Every point is fixed, stereotyped as it were, and they cannot depart from the plan marked out. This course, if continued, will cause them to become narrow-minded, circumscribed in their views, and will soon leave them as destitute of life and energy as are the hills of Gilboa of dew and rain. They must throw the soul open and let the Holy Spirit take possession to impress the mind. When everything is laid out beforehand, and they feel that they cannot vary from the set discourses, the effect is little better than that produced by reading a sermon.

"God would have His ministers wholly dependent upon Him, but at the same time they should be thoroughly furnished unto every good work. No subject can be treated before all congregations in the same manner. The Spirit of God, if allowed to do its work, will impress the mind with ideas calculated to meet the cases of those who need help. But the tame, formal discourses of many who enter the desk have very little of the vitalizing power of the Holy Spirit in them" (*Testimonies to the Church*, Vol. 5, 251).

Isaiah heralded the good news of the Saviour's birth and prophesied His death. He was a notable prophet in Israel who was never afraid to proclaim the word of the Lord. It was not always so in Isaiah's life. In chapter six of the book that bears his name, God revealed Himself to him in a vision. When he beheld the glory of God, he then looked upon himself and said, *Woe is me! For I am lost; for I am a man of unclean lips, for my eyes have seen the King, the Lord of hosts! (Verse 5).*

God must have been pleased that Isaiah saw the sinfulness of his condition and a willingness to change. For God proceeded to empower him to be His mouthpiece. *Then flew one of the seraphim to me, having in his hand a burning coal which he had taken with tongs from the altar. And he touched my mouth, and said; "Behold, this has touched your lips; your guilt is taken away, and your sins forgiven." And I heard the voice of the Lord saying, "Whom shall I send, and who will go for us?" Then I said, "Here am I! Send me!"* (Isaiah 6:6–8).

For Isaiah to experience the power of the Holy Spirit, he had to see himself, bare and empty before the Lord. He had to see his sinfulness and the need for the cleansing power of God. Isaiah was called and empowered by God for his mission. God is still calling men and women to fulfill His mission to the world. We dare not go without His power to accomplish the task. His power is available to all those who will humble their hearts and invite Him in. We are carrying the last message of mercy to a perishing world, and God calls upon us to bring freshness and power into our work. We can do this only by the aid of the Holy Spirit" (*Testimonies to Ministers*, 313).

This has been a refreshing experience for me and I too need this divine power to bear witness for Him in my daily living and sermonizing. As I stand before men and women I feel His divine anointing and I know it must be the Holy Spirit's power. This must be the experience of all who bear witness of His name to the world.